Elizabeth Joy

The discovery, shortly after her birth, that
Elizabeth Joy had Down's syndrome was a
terrible shock. Her parents had hoped their
first child would be normal, healthy,
intelligent. Now their dream was shattered. In
the first anxious days they wondered if it
would be difficult to love her. Why had this
happened to them? How different would she
be?

This book is a mother's story – an honest
account not only of the problems caused by
handicap but also of how suffering can be seen
as a special kind of blessing. Despite the pain
and tears there is throughout a sense of God's
love and care and the realization that
Elizabeth Joy is a special gift, born to bring
joy.

For Mark and Elizabeth
    without whom this book could not
    have been written

For our parents and our friends
    who have shared in the tears and the joy

For Nicholas
    who is a new part of the rest of our life

Elizabeth Joy

CAROLINE PHILPS

A LION PAPERBACK

Tring · Belleville · Sydney

Copyright © 1984 Caroline Philps

Published by
Lion Publishing plc
Icknield Way, Tring, Herts, England
ISBN 0 85648 576 4
Albatross Books
PO Box 320, Sutherland, NSW 2232, Australia
ISBN 0 86760 493 X

Published in co-operation with the Down's Children's Association,
4 Oxford Street, London W1

First edition 1984
Reprinted 1984 (twice)

Bible quotations from the *Good News Bible*,
copyright 1966, 1971 and 1976 American Bible Society,
published by the Bible Societies/Collins

Phototypeset by Input Typesetting Ltd., London
Printed and bound in Great Britain by
Collins, Glasgow

Contents

A poem for Elizabeth

Who is it who was there
And here
And there
Before there was any place,
Before there was a need for time,
Who was it,
Before even the universe itself was,
Alpha and Omega
Yet unconfined by beginning or end,
Unborn and undying,
Not travelling but being,
Boundless,
For whom all space is but the space
between his fingers;
Who knew me and all my days
Before there was a man,
Before there was a world;
Who is it
Who holds the moon in place
And hides an oak tree in an acorn?
Is this the one
Whose child I am, who takes me on his knee?
Am I to reason with him?
Who am I but to kneel before him?
And if he should love me,
Is that not all I need?

By Michael Hollow
– written after he heard about the birth
of Elizabeth in June 1981

Introduction

It is our hope and prayer that *Elizabeth Joy* will be of help
to different people. Those with Down's children may find it
easiest to identify with the feelings and problems we have
found but we hope too that parents of children with other
handicaps may gain something of value from the book, as
well as those involved or interested in the care of
handicapped children and their parents. And of course we
hope that the general reader who has no particular personal
or professional concern with handicapped children will
enjoy the book too.

Down's children vary enormously in their potential:
some are fortunate enough to achieve a measure of
independence, while others are never able to do this. We
hope that readers will not be too concerned to compare
their child's progress with that of Elizabeth. The stress on
her progress in the account of the first year of her life
reflects my difficulty in coming to terms with her limitations
rather than any intrinsic value we would place on her
ability to achieve. We hope instead that the reader will be
able to see each child as an individual created to offer
something unique to the world. This must be true of all
types of handicap, not just Down's syndrome. Perhaps the
following passage from Morris West's *The Clowns of God*
expresses something of this: 'I know what you are
thinking. You need a sign. What better one could I give
than to make this little one whole and new? I could do it;
but I will not. I am the Lord and not a conjuror. I gave
this mite a gift I denied to all of you – eternal innocence.
To you she looks imperfect – but to me she is flawless, like
the bud that dies unopened or the fledgling that falls from
the nest to be devoured by the ants. She will never offend
me, as all of you have done. She will never pervert or

destroy the work of my Father's hands. She is necessary to you. She will evoke the kindness that will keep you human. Her infirmity will prompt you to gratitude for your own good fortune. More! She will remind you every day that I am who I am, that my ways are not yours, and that the smallest dust mote whirled in darkest space does not fall out of my hand. I have chosen you. You have not chosen me. This little one is my sign to you. Treasure her!'

Although Mark has not actually written any of the book, it is his book too, to the extent that he has shared closely in the events and emotions described. Perhaps men find it harder to quantify and explain their feelings than women, nor is it so necessary, because often the father of a handicapped child is not daily confronted with normal children and their parents and is therefore one step removed from the continuous battle to come to terms with one's child's limitations. Or at least this has been the case with us. It may also be easier for a father to accept a handicapped daughter than a son because his identity is not so closely bound up with her as is a woman's. This is as maybe. It remains a fact that as a couple we have experienced pain and joy together as we have started to learn the special lessons Elizabeth can teach us, and the differences in our feelings and in our approach to problems have enriched the experience for us.

Mark and Caroline Philps

THE FIRST YEAR

1

A Special Gift

Saturday 11th April

I couldn't sleep for ages last night. I suppose I must have eventually drifted off as I remember waking up again thinking it might all be a very bad dream, and then the sickening thud at the pit of my stomach told me it wasn't.

I'm glad the sun was shining and I could, see a large expanse of grass from my first-floor window. If it had been raining it would all have been much harder to bear. And yet I couldn't wait to be allowed to walk down to the special baby-care unit to see my own small daughter. I could only have held her for half an hour altogether in the first twenty-four hours of her life: that was so terribly frustrating.

I'd cried a lot last night – a nurse brought me in some tea and said, 'You'll be alright, you've got faith haven't you?' Why were one's personal beliefs suddenly everyone else's property? How did she know it would be so easy? She continued, 'They don't know who brings them up anyway.' Was this meant to be consoling? I'm so glad I spent two university vacations working at a hospital for mentally-handicapped children and also knew one little girl well – this was far better than just reading a description of her illness in a book. I knew without doubt that they do know who cares for them and who loves them.

As I arrived in the special baby-care unit I felt very excited and also apprehensive. Would I love her? Would the gap of time when I hadn't seen her put a barrier between us? Could I accept her? Why did I have to fight the feeling of revulsion and alienation when I thought that her body wasn't made in quite the same way as ours?

Yet there she was – such a tiny creature. I hated the stockinette cap and mittens taped onto her hands, the aertex nightie that swamped her. It made her more alien. I wanted to cuddle her, and the hat always fell off or into her eyes. She was wrapped up tightly in a sheet and given to me to hold. I felt very angry when I heard she had cried for half an hour when they'd been too busy to feed her. I wanted to be here with her. I sat in a chair in a room full of incubators and held her close and talked to her. A sister came up later and told me I would tire her out. How could love tire someone out? Someone who needed all the love there is, I thought fiercely. I wanted to make up for not being allowed to be with her. She was my little daughter, not government property.

She reminded me of my great-grandmother. The moment she was born I seemed to see her face – was it the slightly shrivelled appearance of new babies or the little, straight, closed mouth over no teeth? I fought back the tears – maybe they were relief – I knew I loved her. It was heaven to hold her close to me. I hated having to put her back in her cot but she was very tiny and I was told she needed to rest.

Was it only last night that the paediatrician had wanted to see my husband? The nurse had told me this when I first went to see my new daughter at 5 p.m. I thought then that there must be something wrong and I looked down at the tiny person in my arms: an expression, or was it the shape of her face, reminded me of something. And then I knew. 'She's a mongol isn't she?' I said to the nurse. 'They don't know yet' she replied. But I knew. I bravely said that I was a Christian and God must have a good purpose in giving her to us. The nurse praised my attitude, but I said to my daughter, 'You'll be the brainiest mongol out', and I tried hard not to cry.

Mark came as soon as I'd managed to telephone him – I hated telling him over the phone – I felt guilty about that. He'd just been phoning our family and friends to tell them we had a daughter and now he would have to phone again. I felt I'd failed him. I hadn't managed to have a normal baby like the other mothers in the hospital. I was relieved to discover that Mark had spent half an hour with her when I was being stitched up. He hadn't noticed anything wrong then and just thought she was a very sweet little baby. I sensed that he already loved her despite everything. But I tried to be brave for him.

The paediatrician arrived and told us we possibly had a Down's baby. I hated the label then. It made it hard to think of her as a person. He was sending off blood samples for tests and we would know within a week. He was caring, yet it seemed so easy for someone else to talk about something that had just completely changed our lives.

Sunday 12th April

I was allowed to move down to the special baby-care unit today. I couldn't believe that I could have my daughter with me all the time. I just lay on the bed and listened to her breathing . . . it was so amazing to think she belonged to me. She had such tiny hands and face.

I read my Bible for the first time since she was born. I read Psalms 61 and 62, the Bible reading for that day, and one verse jumped out at me from the page: 'You have heard my promises, O God, and you have given me what belongs to those who honour you.' That was how I was meant to understand our little daughter, as a gift, a special gift. We had thought we would call a daughter Sarah, but somehow it didn't fit. As I thought, I felt that we should call her Elizabeth, Elizabeth Joy. Elizabeth because this means 'gift or promise of God', and Joy because I knew we should be confident that she would bring us much joy. It was an act of faith at this moment but we could be sure God would honour that faith in him and in our daughter. I went on to read, 'God is my strong protection and my shelter, his love is constant.' I felt I knew the truth of this verse in hospital now. I felt very vulnerable, and yet I knew that underneath me and around me were the strong arms of God. He would keep me holding on to him. I couldn't pray and yet I sensed I was with God all the time and that somehow it didn't matter.

Wednesday 15th April
I have felt today as if I've become the butt between the conflicting ideas of the two sisters in charge of the ward. They do not seem to agree about how Elizabeth should be fed, how many times I should try to breast-feed and how many bottle or tube-feeds she should have. I can't cope with it. The pressure to get her to suck seems so great, it feels as if she will never be able to come home. Yet at midnight tonight I tried to feed her myself and she tried so hard to suck the nipple. She started crying because she was so frustrated that she couldn't succeed. Or at least that was how it seemed to me. I was thrilled that she should exhibit such normal emotions.

Today I felt really grateful that Elizabeth has Down's syndrome and not something else. A doctor introduced me to a family whose daughter has Cri du Chat syndrome. It is a severe handicap and there is no chance that the baby can survive for very long. She has to be almost constantly in special care. It seemed wise of the doctor to introduce us. I felt sorry for the parents . . . they were obviously still very upset even though the baby is a few weeks old. It helped to put our own problems into perspective.

Mark's mother arrived this afternoon. It was so lovely to see her. Almost as soon as she and Mark arrived she suggested she might buy Elizabeth a crib to come home to, and they rushed off before the shops shut. I was thrilled as it was good to get Elizabeth something special. Most of the equipment I have is second-hand and it seems to matter more that she has nice things. I think perhaps I am fearful of the idea of treating handicapped people as second-class citizens. I am really looking forward to seeing Mark's mother tomorrow . . . there's so much to tell her.

Thursday 16th April. Maundy Thursday

Today I came to the end of myself. I couldn't cope any more. Perhaps intellectually I'd accepted Elizabeth's birth in the first few days. It hit my heart today. Yet I didn't have to cope. I phoned Mark at 7.30 a.m. to beg his mother to come soon. I was desperate. I knew somehow that she would understand how I felt. Her first child died after a few months: she had been severely handicapped. I felt very close to Mark's mother now.

After lunch the drugs that I'd been given to help my womb contract properly began to act rather powerfully. I was unprepared for this and panicked. I was waiting on tenterhooks too, because I felt sure I'd overheard the doctor talking about whether I could go home with Elizabeth. I couldn't bear the suspense. I thought I was going to pass out. 'I can't stand it any more, any more' I yelled at the nurse who brought me some pain-killers. I felt very angry that I hadn't been warned the drugs would make me feel awful and that all I needed was to take something with them. Why hadn't anyone told me?

It was amazing how closely my feelings appeared to be mirrored in the Bible reading for today, from Psalm 39: '. . . my suffering only grew worse, and I was overcome with anxiety. The more I thought, the more troubled I became; I could not keep from asking: Lord, how long will I live?' When I was told that I could go home with Elizabeth I just couldn't believe it. I felt like a prisoner being set free . . . or even as if I'd come back from death. This was truly Easter, not just in the time of year but in the events in my life.

As I pulled the huge babygrow onto Elizabeth's tiny floppy limbs I began to dare to think that this really was my little girl and that I was free to look after her in the way I chose now. I needn't live in fear that I wasn't obeying the rules of this nurse or the other and I even could breast-feed her when I wanted to, without being told that I would tire her out. Perhaps my life was beginning again.

2

Transition

Thursday 16th April

I was laden with tins of baby-milk formula, vitamins and instructions about making up feeds. I tottered out of the side door of the hospital into the fresh air. Our car was outside. The sister carried Elizabeth and then gave her to me as I sat in the back seat. It seemed as if I hadn't been in the car for a very long time; it was comfortingly the same old blue Morris with the bit of carpet coming off the dashboard ledge.

As we drove slowly down the road from the hospital I saw people dressed in ordinary clothes pushing push-chairs, crossing at traffic lights. The shop lights were on and the colours seemed so bright.

What exactly had happened to me in hospital? Why did it feel like coming back to the world of the living on this twilight car ride? It seemed that what David, our vicar, had said to me was right. 'People are depersonalized in hospital until they submit to the rules.' I was so afraid of doing anything wrong that I wouldn't step out of line. Was that how we were controlled, made submissive? Perhaps it was dangerous to think like this but it made me feel angry.

But there were nurses who had cared and had talked to me like another human being, about ordinary things: about their weekend off or their fiancé. These conversations had been like a thin thread for me, a thread linking me with the reality that had been my life and my world, a world that I seemed to have lost so suddenly.

I cried as we pulled up outside the house and carried Elizabeth inside. I felt so relieved to be back. It was marvellous to go up to our apple-green carpeted bedroom and to slide under the duvet with Elizabeth beside me in her new brown wicker crib, gentle beige flounces draped over it.

Later I had to make up some feeds. I felt worried about

putting the correct amount of formula into the bottle and adding the water. Why did it seem so difficult? How could I do this every day for months, and were the bottles and teats properly sterilized? This was such a small job; how would I cope with the rest?

17th April. Good Friday
Elizabeth had only one bottle last night. At the next feed she seemed ready to suck the breast and just went on and on. I felt so proud of her. My relief at the prospect of jettisoning the formula and all the instructions was totally disproportionate to the task involved. I was elated. But today I began to lose confidence again.

The midwife arrived just when I was beginning to panic. I felt then that God is kind in his timing of things. It was comforting to hear her talk to Elizabeth so naturally and to call her Lillybet.

19th April. Easter Sunday
I felt determined to go to church today. It was Easter Sunday. I just had to go and rejoice about the resurrection with the people I'd begun to regard as part of our family.

Rita, the vicar's wife, came to fetch me and we walked in just after the service had begun. We slid quietly into a pew at the back. The familiar words of the communion service felt rock-like and comforting and yet pregnant with fresh meaning.

David preached from part of Paul's second letter to the Corinthians, chapter five. The thrust of his message was: 'At all times we carry in our mortal bodies the death of Jesus, so that his life may be seen in our bodies . . . death is at work in us', and, 'We fix our attention on things that are unseen.'

Initially I was surprised by the unusual nature of the passage for a day when we were rejoicing in the resurrection; in Jesus conquering death. Yet it was amazingly relevant to our experience.

What does it mean to 'carry in our mortal bodies the death of Jesus so that his life may be seen in us'? David explained about our need to 'die' to the world – just as Jesus

15

had died. Yet for us it would not be a physical death but a turning away from all the values we held so dear: intellectual achievement, sophistication, material gain, ambition, possessions, independence. Then we could live a new life, a life in which Jesus Christ and·his life of love and self-giving and goodness could be seen.

I became a Christian while I was still at secondary school. It meant a great change for me. I had found someone who prayed to Jesus and had, it appeared to me, a friendship with him. I'd never encountered this before. My friend had a peace and a sense of direction that I lacked.

For several months I struggled with the fear of becoming someone I didn't want to be – perhaps a terrible kind of pious goody-goody, not a real human at all. Then I began to feel that Christianity still had the only possible answer. It was the answer to the feelings I had of guilt at not living my life the way I wanted to live it. I never could attain the standards I set myself. I felt far away from God and I certainly had no clear sense of direction or purpose.

One evening, after a long walk, I remember going with my friend into her bedroom and kneeling by her bed. I prayed confidently, perhaps for the first time in my life, knowing inside that someone was listening. I prayed to Jesus, a historical person who had lived a human life and yet was also God's Son. I realized that he was alive not just 2,000 years ago, but now today, in a spiritual sense, and he was able to be known by anyone who wanted to know him. I asked him to come into my life, to take control – to show me the plan he had for my life step by step, and to help me to follow it.

Then, I experienced a change. My guilt seemed to be utterly removed and I knew that all I had ever done wrong had been forgiven. Jesus had already paid the price for this wrong by his death on the cross. I felt a deep joy; not bubbly happiness but a peace that has only left me since in times of doubt and depression.

This had felt like a new birth. But now fifteen years later I was experiencing a kind of death. It was a death to all I had hoped for: a normal, healthy, intelligent, beautiful child. Perhaps intelligent had been at the top of the list. We had lost this and lost all the dreams of picnics and painting and sharing little things with someone alive to the newness of it all. Yet perhaps we had gained an opportunity. A chance to experience more of God's plan for all of us. True happiness could only come through having Jesus' values. We had been forced to turn away from the goals of this life to something new.

Jesus said that we must become like little children to enter the kingdom of heaven. What really matters is having a trusting, child-like faith in a loving God. Elizabeth could have this and we could learn from her to have it too — unfettered by the ambitions that many people around us had; ambitions fostered by the media and advertising.

David said in his Easter Sunday sermon that 'at all times' we would carry about this death. Elizabeth would always be with us to remind us of what really mattered to God — love, simplicity, joy. It would be hard sometimes, but the challenge of this opportunity to learn something infinitely worthwhile stayed with me as the sermon ended.

I held Rita's arm as we walked up to the altar to receive communion. I smiled gently at a few of the now familiar faces of the parish Mark had worked in for six months. As we returned to our seats I noticed several people crying. David had announced in the notices earlier in the service that it had now been confirmed that Elizabeth had Down's syndrome. I was moved that people shared in our sadness so genuinely. As we slipped out of church, before the service ended, I felt grateful to be a member of this part of God's family. Perhaps Elizabeth had much to teach all of us — I felt faintly excited at the prospect.

3

A New Beginning

Monday 20th April
I saw a television programme today about a physically-handicapped person. It was part of a series about the meaning of Easter and I found I understood in a new way the kind of triumph over difficulties this woman had experienced. Perhaps Elizabeth was taking us into a larger world.

Preceding this programme there had been a film sequence, showing young children playing in a park. I cried as I watched it, thinking that we might never have this kind of fun with Elizabeth. It was hard to imagine her growing older and being able to walk or talk.

I talked a great deal to Mark's mother; she has been so helpful with the practical things. I didn't realize I'd feel that even knowing the best way to deal with nappies was complicated.

I said something I'd been worrying about since Elizabeth was born. 'No one will try to persuade us to put her into an institution, will they? I feel frightened someone will try to take her away.'

It was a relief to speak these fears out loud. I suppose they are irrational. We are Elizabeth's parents. But fears have deep origins sometimes and these went back ten years to the vacations when I worked at a hospital for mentally handicapped. The hospital has been rebuilt since, but I particularly remembered one of the staff. She had her own problems, I know, but she seemed so callous. I couldn't bear the indignity of a row of large handicapped people seated on pots on a grey stone floor. I expect it is different now and I was an impressionable person then, but the nightmare quality will always remain.

Tuesday 21st April
We had to take Elizabeth back to the hospital today to be weighed. I suppose it was because she was only four-and-a-half pounds when she was allowed home, but I felt it was really to see if I could look after her properly. I experienced an intense feeling of failure when the paediatrician said she had lost weight. In fact, all babies lose weight after beginning to breast-feed and it was less than an ounce, but perhaps the pressure to please the hospital was still in my mind. I felt frightened I might not be allowed to take her home again.

The paediatrician was encouraging about her head control. I gathered that Down's children's muscles are floppy, hypotonic, but Elizabeth seemed to be not too badly affected.

I found it quite painful to go again into the special baby unit and have her weighed in the room in which I had spent last week. Was it only last week? As we carried Elizabeth out to the car I felt the same sense of freedom I had experienced on Thursday. How afraid I am of not holding on to Elizabeth. I suppose that was why I constantly feared she would die while we were in hospital. She did seem so tiny. The shock of having a handicapped child made me expect only worse things to happen. My confidence in a world that was basically orderly had been shaken. Yet in all this I knew too that God is there, and he loves us. It is a strange paradox.

Wednesday 22nd April
I went out to the shops for the first time today. I left Elizabeth at home with Mark's mother. It was cold for the end of April and she was not yet two weeks old. I walked slowly along the High Road, delighting in the sense of freedom it brought me to be in the world again. It still felt as if I'd just come out of prison. I saw people rushing and wondered why they should hurry and couldn't enjoy the grey-blueness of the sky, the pollarded trees beginning to bud and the freedom of each moment.

I wandered into a clothes shop to find some jeans to fit my expanded hips and met a friend from church inside. He didn't recognize me at first. It made me feel strange; almost as if I really had come back from the dead. Once I had spoken to him about Elizabeth he relaxed and talked about her too.

Thursday 23rd April

We had a marvellous letter today. We've had many already from friends since we sent out the birth announcement card with an explanation of Elizabeth's problem. People have sent little dresses and cardigans; I've found it exciting to receive such pretty clothes for her. But this letter has meant a great deal. It was from a friend we met last summer with a Down's girl of four and a half, also called Elizabeth. Her mother said that she would have ten of her Elizabeth for the bridges she had built in her family, marriage and small village community. I shall never forget this because she knows the pain and can still rejoice.

The telephone rang and I answered it for the first time since Elizabeth's birth. I feel as if I am emerging slowly from the protective shell I built around myself. It was a member of the local Down's Society. The consultant paediatrician had said she would give them our number. I didn't feel ready to talk. I felt worried about meeting other people who shared our situation so soon. Perhaps I do not want to admit yet that I am one of them. I still feel frightened I have lost the me of the days before Elizabeth. Maybe I am struggling to find that first, before I venture onto new ground. I said I would like some books and information but wouldn't come to a group meeting just yet. She told me of the support the group had given her; how these people had become some of her best friends. I don't want that. I don't want to be separated from normal families. Elizabeth needs to mix with normal children more than anything. I visualized a kind of 'mother's meeting' and pompously said that my husband was very involved too but I'd phone when I felt able to see her.

She said she expected life seemed very black at the moment, but I don't really feel that. We do get times when we cry, but it is still very exciting to have a tiny baby to feed and dress and get to know. I told her I was a Christian and that helped me, but I know I didn't give her a chance. She seemed very understanding and yet I was on the defensive.

I still need to protect myself, the hurt and wounded 'me' inside. I can't go very fast into the reality of it all.

As I put the phone down I heard Elizabeth cry – a tiny cry almost like a cat crying. Yet it thrilled me with excitement and I rushed upstairs, forgetting about my raised blood pressure and the need to go slowly. This gut response to another tiny human was so novel. I looked forward intensely to picking her up and feeding her, knowing she needed me.

When she is wakeful she has been in the Mr Men bouncing cradle I made before her birth. It is exciting to see her become part of the family and peep out from the edge of the huge red sleeping-suit with her bright blue eyes.

All her clothes are so huge. The sleeping-suit is wrapped around her like a blanket. Mark's cousin sent a parcel of tiny clothes today. Her daughter was premature. At least now there is a chance I can find something that will fit her. Why do I mind so much about her clothes? I want her to look like other babies. They always seem to fit into their clothes properly.

Friday 24th April
Elizabeth is two weeks old today. A friend we'd first met when Mark was at theological college in Nottingham phoned to ask if she could come and stay for the weekend. She wanted to help with Elizabeth. She is a midwife and an expert at breast-feeding techniques. It seemed again that God was providing just what we needed at the right time. Mark's mother had returned home yesterday and we missed her a great deal, despite feeling we had to learn to cope on our own. To have Jane, someone with whom we had shared a lot in the past few years, made me feel more confident.

She arrived with some books, the first I had seen on Down's syndrome. Mark had been to the library while I was still in hospital to find something factual about it, but I suppose I hadn't wanted to read anything then. Reading about Down's syndrome now was still disturbing, although I wanted to find out all I could. I was frightened of reading something I couldn't cope with.

Apparently, Down's syndrome is caused in 97 per cent of cases at conception, when the egg is fertilized. For some reason, at present unknown, an extra chromosone attaches itself to the twenty-first pair of chromosones. Down's syndrome is thus known as Trisomy 21. The extra chromosone causes certain physical characteristics. Most Down's children have some of these although not necessarily all of them.

Elizabeth's eyes are slanted slightly upwards and the bridge of her nose is flattened. Her nasal passages are rather narrow and this explains the snuffly noises she has made since birth. I remember in hospital lying listening to the raspy noise she made. It was worse when she was being tube-fed and had a tube permanently up her nose. I eventually begged the doctor to remove the tube, except for feeding, because the noise seemed to be getting worse. It was a pathetic sound then, but now it was less noticeable and I had become used to it. I hope when she gets older she will lose it, but I find it very hard to imagine her getting older.

Her hands do not have the single palmer crease common to many Down's children, but they are quite square. Her head is not flattened at the back as is also common, but her arms and legs and neck are shorter and her head smaller than average. Perhaps this is the reason that her clothes don't really fit.

Her tongue doesn't seem very large to me, but it does pop out from her mouth sometimes. Her circulation must be poor as her hands and feet get cold very easily. I hope as she grows bigger that this will improve as she has to wear many layers of clothes at the moment. Sometimes I resent our cold house and fear it will harm Elizabeth. But I know God led us clearly to this job and the house belongs to it, so I will have to trust him about the house.

I was surprised as I continued to read to discover that Down's syndrome occurs on average in one out of every 600 live births. I hadn't realized it was so common. Was that because people hide their handicapped children away and we don't meet them in the street, or was I just inordinately sensitive about that? The frequency increases with age so that by the time the mother is forty-five years old the risk has increased to one in fifty. I found it reassuring to realize then that we were in no way responsible for this genetic abnormality. I was only twenty-eight and the risk was about one in 2,000 at this age. I knew that nothing we did could have made any difference. In some way it made me more aware that God was in control.

The book I was reading, *Improving Babies with Down's Syndrome* by Rex Brinkworth and Joseph Collins, explained about the value of early stimulation for Down's babies. Apparently much can be achieved if games and exercises are systematically carried out with them from birth. When I went up to change Elizabeth later on I tried out some of the exercises suggested. I laid her on the changing-mat, lifted her feet one at a time and gently dropped them. This was to encourage her to prevent them falling back and to kick. I pushed on the soles of her feet towards the knee in a gentle walking action and then tickled and stroked the soles of her feet to encourage a response. Pulling her gently up by her arms, supporting her neck, I was pleased to see she was beginning to improve the way she held up her head.

I rolled her onto her stomach and bent her legs into a crawling position. Pushing on the soles of her feet I encouraged her to move up the mat towards her furry bunny rattle which I'd placed at the end.

I felt really excited that here was something I could do to help her and planned to try these exercises every change time.

I began to gain the impression that Elizabeth was not too severely affected by Down's syndrome. She did not lie staring at the ceiling without crying as was the description of a typical baby. She sucked well although she choked on her feeds. It can be difficult on occasions to breast-feed a Down's baby successfully, but we seemed to be progressing well. I was so grateful for this. The antibodies in the milk must help her develop some resistance to illness. I was frightened by the continued references to Down's children's general lack of resistance to illness. I had visions of a permanently sick child, and could only hope that the milk would help.

A line in the first chapter caught my attention: 'We pray that this book will reach every parent in need. We hope they will then do something. It was St Teresa who said: "Prayer consists not in much thinking but in much loving." '

23

The other book, *Small Ship, Great Sea* by T. de Vries-Kruyt, was also encouraging. It was the life-story of a Down's boy. I read it rapidly, rejoicing in the positive attitude of his parents and the joy and love he brought. Their faith had helped them to care for him, but perhaps more remarkably Jan Maarten's own very real faith had helped them too. In the prologue, his father wrote:

It is to help others find the happiness that can rise out of great sorrow that I shall try to answer the question 'how is it Jan Maarten is what he is?' . . . His upbringing was based largely on what we discovered in the child himself.

The conclusion to the book was moving.

How did Jan Maarten always manage to transform our grief and to put us on the track of 'being happy together' in such unexpected ways? With his limited mental capacity and his great heart he had all that is really essential to human happiness. His special way of looking at people and things meant so much to us that our daily life now seems almost colourless without him.

He lived in *our* world in so far as he was able. But the miracle was that he opened up *his* world to us so easily, a world where warmth, humour and sheer happiness reigned and where all activity was directed towards a single goal: how and in what way could he help everyone today?

Jan Maarten was permitted to live among us for far longer than we ever dared hope; and for this we shall always be grateful.

I gained fresh hope for Elizabeth as I read. I had been worried that as she grew up she would be harder to handle but Jan Maarten learnt well what he was allowed to do and he was a very polite, manageable child. Nothing I read about him gave me cause to fear the future. I began instead to feel that the three of us had embarked on an adventure.

It seemed to me a privilege that what we read and put into practise could help Elizabeth to develop. I felt that though her handicap was so permanent, enabling her to fulfil her own potential was an ongoing challenge and an ever-changing situation. The responsibility sometimes felt great and yet we were not alone. If God had entrusted her to us, he would help us to do our best.

4

Facing Reality

Tuesday 26th April
The results of our blood tests have arrived and the hospital asked us to come in to see them. When Elizabeth was born and I had realized there was a 5 per cent chance that Down's syndrome was hereditary, I began to feel this must be so in our case. I had lost my faith in statistics. We had a Down's child, despite the odds against it, why not go the whole way? It was no good thinking that it only happened to everyone else. I had to face the possibility that Elizabeth could be our only child and she was handicapped. I had always wanted three children. Sometimes the prospect of having no normal children seemed bleak; as if the only record of our lives left on earth when we died would be someone not quite as we were; not developing the gifts we'd always wanted to have, not marrying and continuing our lives in those of her children. I in no way believe in reincarnation but I suppose I feel we pass on to our children much of our essential selves, our personality and our beliefs. I felt frightened at there being no reminders left of our living here. Yet why did this matter? I suppose it is a primitive search for security and immortality that doesn't have much to do with a Christian view of things.

Our real future lies in heaven if we trust God and the Bible assures us that the worthwhile, God-inspired deeds we do and the people we really are, will continue in heaven, transformed by God's power and presence into something far more beautiful. On earth we would be leaving someone who cares about other people, someone who is simple; a reminder of God's standards. That would be a fitting memorial; perhaps a better memorial than we deserved.

I knew that the mother was responsible for the faulty chromosones if Down's syndrome was inherited. I felt relieved about this. I couldn't bear to add another burden to the sadness Mark's mother had already suffered in her past.

We arrived at the hospital feeling apprehensive. Nothing had grown from the culture of blood cells. We could have other normal children. Elizabeth's birth had been 'one of those things'. The relief was exhilarating. It was great to phone our parents with good news instead of bad.

Friday 29th April
The hospital again today, this time for an early postnatal check. I didn't really know why I had been asked to come and the obstetrician didn't seem to know either. Her opening words were, 'Why have you come?' I suppose she then looked more closely at my notes and saw the details about Elizabeth. I said hastily that the registrar had made the appointment, not myself, and she told me she wanted to see how I was getting on psychologically. By this time I was not feeling very sympathetic towards her.

She seemed convinced I would blame the hospital for Elizabeth's birth, carefully explaining that if I'd been over thirty-eight I would automatically have been tested. I said it would have made no difference; that I was a Christian and believed we'd been given Elizabeth for a reason. But she insisted that next time I was pregnant I would certainly want an amniocentesis. My denial did not persuade her.

She then suggested that the best thing to do now would be to go off and have another child soon. She also told me of a Down's girl she had heard about who had a normal baby. But she must surely have been mosaic, in other words, with only a few of her cells affected by an extra chromosone, otherwise it would have been impossible for her to have a normal child.

I felt elated as I walked out to join Rita, who had kindly brought Elizabeth and me to the appointment. The idea of more children seemed exciting. Yet later as I thought over what had been said I felt it was really a way of not accepting the present moment. It would be no good trying to have a 'replacement' as soon as possible. It would mean never really coming to terms with Elizabeth herself.

The paediatrician too had spoken to us about having other children, but he had said he'd always suggested to bereaved parents (and in some sense we were bereaved) that they have a time gap of two years until they had worked through their grief. This seemed a more realistic approach.

My parents arrived this afternoon to stay for a few days. They hadn't come for long before because we were too upset to cope with each other. They had spent about half an hour at the hospital when Elizabeth was three days old, but Mummy especially had found it very hard. I remember her saying how sad she felt that I would never have an adult relationship with Elizabeth as she did with me. I think that says a great deal about how much she values our relationship, and I was touched.

It seemed clear how much God is in control of the timing of everything. It had been marvellous that Elizabeth arrived three weeks early. Mark's only holiday at this time of year had then fallen in the week I came out of hospital. Now Mum and Dad had come at a time when I felt able to cope with some of the everyday jobs, and was less emotional. Dad has promised to put some new locks on the doors; I feel more vulnerable with a tiny baby and Mark out a great deal. Mum has got the cooking under control.

Elizabeth has drawn us closer together than we've been before. We were able to have a long talk tonight and to share things I would not have thought of saying before: things that matter about our shared past, about the meaning of life, our faith in God and his reality in our lives. Mum reminded me that the week before Elizabeth was born they had stayed for the weekend. I had said then that we might have to be prepared for the baby to have something wrong with it. I hadn't remembered saying anything. But in the last weeks of the pregnancy I had to fill in kick charts and have tests done to check the functioning of the placenta because the baby hadn't grown. A sense of anxiety had clouded those days.

Strangely, I had never felt I could ask God for a normal baby; I'd always felt he was asking me to be prepared to accept whatever he sent us, as if we were being prepared for Elizabeth for some time. I later discovered that Dad had had a sense of something being wrong too. I remembered last summer when I'd met another Elizabeth, a Down's girl, at a village holiday club we had helped to organize. I had felt strangely envious of her mother during that week.

When Elizabeth was born I caught myself in one lucid moment feeling that I had always wanted her, just the way she was. It gave me a deeper sense of how intimately God is involved in our lives, causing us to meet people that shape our thoughts and feelings – a special kind of preparation.

Friday 13th May

We went shopping today, Elizabeth propped up a little in the pram so she could see out. I pushed cushions around her and a row of plastic men were strung across the pram. I hoped all these things would stimulate her. She liked looking at the plastic men. As we walked along, several people stopped to look at her and spoke to us. Some were strangers. For a reason I can't grasp I felt compelled each time, as on other days, to say, as if in confession, 'But she has Down's syndrome.' Often they didn't understand the term so I explained more reluctantly, 'She's a mongol.' I have grown to dislike this label.

Their comments were only those of admiring passers by: 'What a sweet little baby.' Why do I feel the need to correct them? She *is* sweet after all. I can be proud of her. I am determined not to succumb to keeping my child at home, away from staring eyes, as I've read some people do, or to cross the street with her when I recognize someone. Yet theirs is only an extreme form of the guilt I have expressed and feel deep down. Our feelings are so paradoxical. I know no one is to blame for Elizabeth's condition and I have every reason to thank God for her. Yet I suppose I feel a failure as a mother.

A friend came round to coffee today with a dress for Elizabeth. I really wanted to explain to her how I felt about it all. I think she expected me to be devastated. I told her how God had prepared us for Elizabeth; our student jobs with handicapped children, meeting Elizabeth last summer, the sense of preparation while I was pregnant.

But I wanted to explain what she meant to us now. She stood for values other than those we might normally hold for our children, such as success, intelligence, material affluence. She challenged our twisted view of life and pushed us closer to God's way of valuing people for who they are, not for what they can do.

I had been thinking recently about how we face tragedy. In some ways having a handicapped child was one of the things I had dreaded most when I was pregnant. Yet that very event had turned out to be a great blessing. This must surely be true of other tragedies we fear. It seems to be the way God works in the world. The cross, the death of Jesus, could be viewed as a senseless tragedy, even a mistake. An innocent man who had spent his time healing and preaching and bringing life to people had to die a criminal's death. Yet this was also the ultimate victory. It was the only way our wrongs could be paid for and salvation could come to a world that had turned away from God. And it didn't end there. Jesus rose from the dead; death was conquered for ever for those who trust in him. The most terrible event of history, the death of God's Son, was really the most important and creative ever to occur.

This seems to be how God works in our lives. It isn't simple. We do go through a kind of death, a great loss and suffering and yet God can transform these things into a rich deep experience that helps us to become bigger people.

God was so much involved in the recent tragedy he surely would be in others that might come our way. I had never felt he had deserted me. He was more real in hospital than at many other times in my life. So God was at work to bring joy out of sadness and life out of death. I had certainly already learnt things I could never have learnt without losing the very thing I'd set my heart on: a normal child.

I was reminded of a Bible verse that had always meant a great deal to me since I first became a Christian. It was from Romans chapter 8: 'In all these things we have complete victory through him who loved us! For I am certain that nothing can separate us from his love: neither death, nor life

. . . neither the present nor the future.' Elizabeth's birth underlined again the truth of this verse for me.

Once we have asked God to work in our lives he continues the redemptive, creative process he began when we first trusted that Jesus had dealt with our sins. He will change our characters by using the events in our lives to make us more Christ-like. Often it seems that the very thing we value too highly he has to prize out of our grasp, to show us we don't really need it. All we really need is God himself. Often he replaces what he has taken away with something of greater value. I know I valued intelligence too highly. I had been brought up in a school system and a cultural background where the number of exams passed and the kind of degree you got really mattered. I was grateful that God was giving me a chance to re-think those values.

I remembered the words by St Teresa that a close friend had sent me while I was in hospital:

> Let nothing disturb thee,
> Nothing afright thee;
> All things are passing
> God never changeth;
> Patient endurance
> Attaineth to all things;
> Who God possesseth
> In nothing is wanting,
> Alone God sufficeth.

I felt that part of God's plan for us was to help us to depend on him alone, rather than on many of the things around us which we had thought mattered so much.

I had never spoken so openly to this particular friend before and as we talked in the garden, across Elizabeth's pram, looking at her asleep in the warm sunshine, I felt again that Elizabeth herself was removing barriers and building bridges.

It was good to explain to my friend that she didn't need to feel sad for me, but I appreciated her sympathy. It has been hardest for me when people have not reacted at all. Maybe they don't understand and perhaps they are afraid of saying very much. But to have people react as if I'd said my daughter has a cold makes me feel I must be imagining the pain I feel.

Wednesday 18th May

Elizabeth's medical card arrived today. As I saw the envelope on the kitchen table with 'Miss E. Philps' written across it, I felt slightly sick. Tears came to my eyes. Probably she would never be called anything else. She would never be married and have children. I had known this in theory, but the official form lying there seemed to make it more concrete.

I thought of the fun and adventure of knowing someone so well in a marriage and of sharing all the areas of one's life, the intense moments of joy and pain and the inconsequential ones, the bizarre and the ordered, the holidays and the work. Life can be so rich and full. Yet would the quality of Elizabeth's life be less because she wouldn't grasp all of its intensity of feeling and complexity of meaning? Perhaps not.

Friday 20th May

I went to the hospital again today for my six week postnatal check. I was barely examined as I had been there three weeks before. Foolishly, I peered over to see my notes, when waiting for the doctor to come. I noticed that they said I had been very depressed when I was discharged and had not coped well with hospital.

I felt very angry. I suppose objectively I had been depressed, but it seemed that it was the hospital that had made it hard for me to cope with its rules and pressures.

While in hospital I had to sleep on one ward where I took care of Elizabeth and have my meals on another, two floors above, where mealtimes were never known in advance. I spent the first few days trying to fit into two routines, arriving when the meal was cold or sometimes over, anxious and hungry.

Well-meaning nurses were frequently asking 'What's the matter?' if I appeared to be crying and I was encouraged to go and talk to other mothers rather than stay in my room which was a kind of haven to me.

Added to this had been the emotional battering I had

31

received from the sister on the labour ward. She showed antagonism to us from my arrival on the ward at 3 a.m. It appeared to relate to our attendance at the local National Childbirth Trust antenatal classes and to the fact that we were Christians.

She was cold and sarcastic to me while in labour, leaving us for long periods with no idea of what was happening. A few days after Elizabeth was born she visited me on the special baby-care unit.

It was 9.30 p.m. I had just turned out my light and had stretched exhausted on the bed, wanting to sleep. She walked in.

'You're not asleep, are you' she said. It was more of a statement than a question.

'How many weeks were you?' she asked, referring to my pregnancy.

'Thirty-seven' I replied.

'You were thirty-eight. Arguing again are you?'

She walked over to look at Elizabeth asleep in her cot, so tiny and vulnerable, her face lit by the light in the passage outside.

'This will test your faith,' she said. Did I imagine the note of victory in her voice?

I said firmly, 'She will make it stronger.'

The sister left then and I cried and cried. I found some consolation in Psalm 64, 'I am afraid of my enemies – save my life. . .' No doubt my feelings were heightened by tiredness and the events of the previous few days but I felt as if I had been attacked. I was hurt and very vulnerable.

I pulled myself back to the present and the notes lying before me. Again I felt angry. I had not coped well with hospital. But we had never for one moment wanted anything but to take Elizabeth home and love her. We were not given any credit for this. Now forever on my record was the fact that I hadn't coped. I had failed. Yet why did it matter so much to appear a failure? I suppose it was because it felt like a misrepresentation of the truth.

As we left the hospital I had to see the receptionist. She said how well Elizabeth looked and told me I was so lucky to have the parental support I had; no wonder I was coping well. Once more I felt angry. Of course our parents had been very supportive, and we both came from medical families, but why do people always think they know your circumstances better than yourself? I said that I found being a Christian and knowing God had planned Elizabeth for our good, made a big difference to me, but she didn't seem to hear.

Monday 23rd May
Elizabeth is six weeks old. I began to keep a record of her progress when she reached a month and I have been encouraged when I've looked back to see how much she has changed. She is awake for between six and eight hours on most days so we can play with her for some time. She briefly holds her rattle on her own and sometimes turns to look if I shake it.

She has begun to show pleasure more and more, especially when she is bounced up and down or I go to pick her up from her cradle. We prop her up in her cradle to watch her duck mobile and she looks at it for some time, her eyes moving as the ducks gently swing. She also looks at herself in the mirror.

I was really excited today. Elizabeth was in her high chair, set at a gentle angle to give her support, and she made her soft jingly bell, which I'd put round her wrist, fall off the end of the tray. She did this half a dozen times before she lost interest. It seems a huge breakthrough that she has realized that what she does can affect objects. Maybe this is just a kind of fluke but I don't think so because she repeated it. She showed determination and, most of all, she has shown us how her mind is beginning to work.

Wednesday 25th May
I went to my first meeting of the Down's group. Pat, the visiting mum, had come to see me a few weeks ago. I was delighted to look at some photographs of her Down's son. There was such a family resemblance. I had never realized that Elizabeth would look like us. I had thought the extra chromosone was the major determining factor in her appearance, but in fact she has more of our chromosones, not less.

So she must resemble us to some extent. The photographs showed Philip playing football in the garden, and enjoying the beach. I began to envisage a more normal life for Elizabeth.

Pat brought me a book: *Helping your handicapped baby* by Cunningham and Sloper. It seems to be just what I need. It has detailed ideas for games and exercises from birth to two years, with ways of organizing a stimulation programme. It is especially geared to Down's children and I haven't been able to put it down. It is sensibly and sensitively written.

As I waited for my lift to the meeting, with the carry-cot tipping forwards in my arms, I felt apprehensive. Mark couldn't come as he had a parish meeting. The person who collected me was friendly and everyone was welcoming and seemed interested in Elizabeth. I felt a bit isolated as they knew each other well but I suppose it is always hard to enter a small group.

I had wondered whether I would be discouraged by seeing older children whose features might appear more pronounced. Someone had frightened me by saying the Down's features become more obvious as the children grow up. I wondered if this was really true. I saw very attractive and active children in parent's photographs, always with a family likeness.

The discussion was about nursery schools. It seemed remote to me. I still wonder if Elizabeth will ever need to go to one. Everyday problems were also discussed and I began to feel there might be value in the meetings despite the danger of worrying about your child having the same problems later on. But I wondered, too, if there could be a sense of competition as each child's progress was discussed in turn. Perhaps that was how *I* felt: trying to prove that Elizabeth would never be as badly affected as the other children. Competition is not necessarily wrong if it spurs you on to harder work with your child, but it could create a lot of guilt if you felt the child's progress depended entirely on your own efforts. It seems so complicated and contradictory to sort out my feelings.

I tried to explain to one of the mothers that I believed God had a good purpose in giving us Elizabeth, but I wasn't sure how much I could say. I didn't want to sound glib. They had gone through the same pain and might not feel so confident. All the parents at the meeting had children under five years old. I suppose I had wondered what the parents would be like. Sometimes I had felt as if I was handicapped too. But the parents were smart, young and generally cheerful. They genuinely seemed to care about Elizabeth as a person. I was pleased I had taken her with me. She always gives me a great deal of comfort when she sits on my lap.

I came away, armed with more books, unsure how I really felt, but tentatively thinking that I would go again.

5

The Holiday

We had booked a farmhouse in Devon for two weeks at the end of June. The holiday had been planned well before Elizabeth's birth. We were going to share the house with some of our closest friends and their two-year-old boy. As it turned out, I think they were some of the very few people we could have spent a long time with at this point. Carolyn was someone I felt did understand what it was like for us and she never talked much about her own child's achievements. We were to spend the week preceding the holiday at Mark's mother's house in Cornwall, so Elizabeth was just over two months old when we set off.

The journey to the West Country was the culmination of an extremely traumatic week. My grandfather had been very ill. My parents rushed down to see him in Exmouth and immediately took him to hospital where he died a few days later. I felt terribly sad. I had so wanted him to see Elizabeth. The funeral was planned for the day after we were due in Cornwall so we would be able to go. Despite the sadness I felt God was in control. We could take Elizabeth and perhaps she might be some comfort to my grandmother.

The other trauma was far less important, but for me,

tired after getting up to feed Elizabeth two or three times a night for two months, as well as coping with the pain of it all, it felt like the last straw. We had been waiting about nine months for a Morris Traveller to be renovated by someone we had known in Nottingham. He had lent us other cars in the meantime, but these had not always been reliable. The latest one had problems with its gearbox. I began to dread the thought of the long journey. Why could we not have our own car? It had been promised so often, particularly for this holiday, and it always failed to materialize.

I couldn't cope with the suspense and the unresolved situations. I felt angry and upset. Wasn't having a handicapped child enough? Why did everything else have to go wrong too? Perhaps it was the first time I had been angry with God for what had happened. I panicked as well about organizing the packing for three weeks away. In the end I took far too many clothes for Elizabeth.

Once we left the familiar streets around our home and drove off towards the motorway I began to calm down. We had left at 6 a.m., but it wasn't early enough to avoid the London rush-hour. Nevertheless, we arrived in Exmouth in time for lunch and my parents and grandmother were pleased to see us.

We were right, my grandmother did find that Elizabeth helped her. She held her for a long time. I know she had been upset about Elizabeth's birth, not understanding what it entailed. But those last few weeks must have been filled with anxiety from another source as she had tried to care for my grandfather. She looked older. She had taken a battering.

As we drove on to Cornwall I thought about the way God could be seen to be in control of life and death. My grandmother had had to face two tragedies within two months of each other, yet in some strange way the first event brought comfort at the second. Elizabeth always seemed to bring good with her into the situations that she entered.

I remembered again how upset I had been at the thought of telling my other grandmother about Elizabeth. She had been unwell for some time. She had told me several times during my pregnancy that she prayed she would live long enough to see our baby. I felt it was a cruel thing to deprive someone so frail of what she longed for. Yet when I told Mark's mother how I felt, she had said she was sure God knew what we needed to learn. Perhaps this would be the last special lesson before she died. God would enable her to bear it.

Encouraged by that thought, I was thrilled and humbled to receive a letter from my grandmother. She said how much she was looking forward to seeing Elizabeth and how much joy she was sure she would bring. She believed she was a very special baby. My mother had written several explanatory letters which had doubtless helped her to understand, but I felt, too, that perhaps we underestimate the strength that older people possess; strength tempered by the trials they have already suffered. Whenever she talked about Elizabeth she always called her 'our baby' and I thanked God for her simple trusting acceptance of a child that others found hard to accept.

We returned to Exeter the next day for the funeral and then began to relax a little as we drove back to the soft grey-green world of Cornwall. I loved to walk down the muddy uneven lane to the ford with the pale green lichen clinging to the branches and Mark's mother's dogs rushing up and down the banks. Elizabeth was happy in the kangaroo pouch and often went to sleep as we jogged up and down. We began to feel just as we had always done when we had retreated to Mark's mother's house, away from the rush of our lives. The peace and quiet and soporific air always had a renewing effect and, more especially on this holiday, it began to help us feel like an ordinary family again. We didn't have to keep explaining to anyone about Elizabeth's problems. We were not seen as an oddity. We had continuity with the past and with the lives we lived before she was born.

It was a relief to be able to talk to Mark's mother about Elizabeth. She understood. We didn't have to explain anything. She too found comfort in cuddling Elizabeth. We had brought a baby bouncer with us which could be hung from the door-frame. Now that Elizabeth could hold her head up quite well we strapped her in and enjoyed seeing her swing about and push herself round with her feet. She smiled and obviously found it was fun. The instructions suggested a baby should be ready for the bouncer at three months, or before if he could hold his head up. In something at least Elizabeth was in step.

We were sad to leave the beautiful greystone house to move on to Devon but we were looking forward to joining Carolyn and Mike. When we arrived there was a pot of tea waiting for us on the large yellow table by the Aga and some flowers put there by the owner. A welcome sign. Anthony was an interesting two-year-old with a very definite personality. He had already developed a liking for books and letters. He took time to accept us and Elizabeth but when he let me join in his games I felt he had paid me a huge compliment.

Sometimes I found myself thinking that Elizabeth would never be like him – she wouldn't develop the subtleties of personality or the ability to play games with words which he so delighted in. It made me sad, yet only fleetingly. I began to appreciate both the children for their differences and individuality. Carolyn helped me with this, spending time 'talking' to Elizabeth. We were excited at the way she was beginning to use sounds: 'ooh, aye, ling, ee, b, m, g'. In the way that babies do, she seemed to hold conversations with us, and she smiled a great deal. By the end of the first week Anthony was noticing Elizabeth too and played nearby as she swung around in the doorway. It was good to see her flex her legs and push up and down with her small feet clad in tiny knitted boots.

She discovered the delights of the large bath on holiday, floating up and down and splashing with her arms and legs. 'Paddling' in warm rock-pools seemed to please her too. There were not many sunny days but we showed her as much as we could, encouraging her to feel the sand with her toes and to watch the sea ebb and flow.

Indoors, she lay on her tummy on a blanket and began to hold her head up well. She started pushing her bottom and legs into the air as if she was trying to crawl. Sometimes she made efforts to roll. She made a lot of progress while we were on holiday. I've noticed since how a complete change in environment always produces real strides in her development, as if she gets bored and stale at home. I suppose we all need a break sometimes.

Each day we played peep-bo, putting a cloth over her face, and she learnt to pull it off by herself. She began to play more definitely with the pram people suspended across the carry-cot and the suction toy we placed on the table at mealtimes. Elizabeth also learnt to sleep through from 9 p.m. to 6 a.m. I began to feel more rested and it meant that on some evenings Mark and I could escape for a late walk along the cliffs or to a local harbour. These were special times; the first times we'd been out alone since it all began.

Mark had some new photographic equipment and it was fun to experiment as the sun began to set over the sea. We scrambled up cliffs and lay headlong on top of them, looking at the streaks of gold in the darkening sky. It was deserted and beautiful. A place in which to be ourselves; a place where no one else could come.

In the daytime we took picnics to waterfalls and wooded walks; explored cliff paths strewn with all kinds of coastal flowers. One day we drove along the coast and watched army manoeuvres on a beach, eating our sandwiches with yachts and windsurfers shooting past. The sense of escape and freedom was always there. On the two Sundays we went to a church where no one knew us or expected anything of us, and this was part of the freedom.

We could pretend that nothing was wrong. We were just an ordinary family pushing a baby around the shops or sitting on the beach. Perhaps we were escaping from reality, but it seemed essential for us at this time, in order for us to go back to it when we returned home. It was easy to enjoy Elizabeth for herself without external reminders of her problem. I felt more like a real mother. I wonder anyway if part of the escape was simply from endlessly comparing Elizabeth with babies of a similar age or with the charts in my baby book. Shouldn't we enjoy any child just for being themselves?

It had been so difficult at first when friends arrived with their babies, born at the same time as Elizabeth. I had felt as if I had nothing in common with them. It had surprised me when they had mentioned nappies or feeding and I had realized I was doing similar things. I'd quite often comment that we had to expect Elizabeth to be different. I was always surprised to discover how her behaviour was like that of all the other babies. In hospital I remember asking several mothers if their babies were normal. Looking back, it seems a crazy thing to have asked. I suppose I was searching for someone else in the same situation: someone to share the isolation with. I felt unlike all other mothers, as if I'd never 'made it'. This feeling took a long time to disappear but the holiday helped.

Although the holiday was an escape I remember in particular standing one day on the edge of Ilfracombe harbour watching a coach empty of passengers. I began to realize that the passengers were all handicapped. I couldn't take my eyes off them. I knew I shouldn't stare yet I felt compelled to keep looking. Was it to see if any of them looked like Elizabeth, or as Elizabeth would in twenty years time? There were several with Down's syndrome and, strangely perhaps, they seemed by far the most attractive and the most normally behaved. I felt relieved. It seemed as if I was looking at people quite familiar to me, no longer strangers whom I feared. Elizabeth had brought us a special link with these unknown people. Although they would never know it, I had my own reason for especially loving them.

6

The Portage Programme

I first heard about the Portage programme when Pat, from the Down's Society, visited me. She mentioned it as some kind of weekly assessment. I was initially horrified at the idea, thinking it would put great pressure on us if Elizabeth seemed to be losing ground. But I had misunderstood completely. I was told there was a waiting list but that the Portage scheme would help Elizabeth if she could get on to the programme.

A few weeks later, a friend from church, a nursery nurse at the local clinic, happened to be with the health visitor when I took Elizabeth to be weighed. She asked me if I wanted to have Portage for Elizabeth. By then I had found out more and said 'yes' immediately. So Chris arrived a few days later with some information and the first activity charts. Elizabeth was six weeks old.

Apparently, Chris had never been interested in handicapped children, but had seen a notice announcing a Portage training course to be held locally in the September before Elizabeth was born – at about the same time that we moved to the parish. Chris dismissed the idea but strangely, in a communion service three weeks later, she felt very sure God was wanting her to do the training. She knew no handicapped children and had no special interest, yet felt it was right to go ahead.

After the course she went to help a physically and mentally-handicapped child. Each week she spent an hour at the child's home, suggesting games and exercises to be carried out which were related to a developmental check-list. The games were to be played about five times a day by the mother or other family members, who were given clear written instructions on a chart. The results were recorded regularly. At the end of each week Chris would assess with the mother how the learning was progressing and would then suggest the next step.

The checklist was divided into different skill areas: infant stimulation (up to about three months), self help (feeding, dressing etc.), motor (sitting, walking), cognitive (work with objects and books) and language. One or two areas might be concentrated on each week, each step broken down into smaller teachable fragments.

It seemed an excellent scheme and when Chris explained it I realized how closely it linked with the ideas in *Helping your handicapped baby*, the book which had seemed so helpful. I was encouraged by the way she had been led towards the programme, and the fact that we knew each other already and that she lived close by, made it an ideal arrangement. She was more than happy to take on Elizabeth and we could both see clearly how God had provided help for Elizabeth even before she was born. It was a lifeline to me.

It was encouraging to be able to talk about Elizabeth's progress in detail, and to be aiming at extending her skills with someone else there to support and help us. I always looked forward to Chris's visits and began to feel they were a priority time in my week. We started with the section covering infant stimulation, recording whether Elizabeth turned to look at a rattle shaken on either side of her head. We moved on to helping her to look at herself in the mirror, to play peep-bo and to crawl. There were many different activities as the weeks passed.

Some weeks seemed discouraging if there were few successes to record, but a highlight for me was when Elizabeth had learnt an activity and we could tick it off on the main checklist, with the date on which she had learnt the skill. To begin with I was too eager to tick off skills. The educational psychologist visited us to help set some long-term goals; skills to be learnt over the next three months. He tested Elizabeth at a few activities and it wasn't always clear if she had learnt them properly. Performing an activity once or twice was not the same as consistently being successful at it. It was an indication to me of my difficulty in accepting her handicap. I so wanted her to succeed. I was affected by the world's view of accepting people only if they are successful. It has taken many months to be less influenced by that view. Perhaps we will never cease to care that our child is retarded. But it seems easier to accept her limitations as she grows older and her personality becomes clearer.

Chris told me of another Portage training course to be run when Elizabeth was about five months old. Mothers were invited and I felt excited at the possibility of learning more about it for myself. To go out on my own and attend a few lectures seemed a great treat. Mark and Chris promised to look after Elizabeth between them. It was the first time I had left her for so long while she was awake and missed giving her a meal, but it worked out reasonably happily for Elizabeth. For me it was a stimulus. I felt an individual again, learning something new yet also something relevant to our situation. Was it my being a teacher that made me so much enjoy being taught myself?

The background to Portage is interesting and helped me

42

understand the programme better. The scheme had arrived in Great Britain six years earlier from Portage, Wisconsin, USA, and is intended for all 'educationally delayed' children. The teaching method is based on behaviour modification. Praise is the major reward and demonstration and prompting are the ways to teach the skills. Another essential process is the breaking down of the skills into tiny parts which a child can learn slowly.

I was saddened by one description of how long it took to teach a child to wash and dry his hands and face. I wondered if I could cope with this each time Elizabeth had something new to learn. But it hasn't been like that. She has taken many weeks to learn some skills but has learnt others in the meantime. Teaching a child you love brings rewards, not despair, and I do not find I am counting the weeks she takes to learn something.

One of the secrets of the success of the Portage programme for parents is the setting of concrete activities to do each day. The child's progress can also be clearly seen on the checklist. It is a very positive approach. Only the skills a child has learnt are recorded, not the skills he cannot attain. There is a guideline to the mental age to which the skills belong, but it is not specific and allows for the natural variations between children. It seems a healthy, helpful way to look at a child's progress.

A year after the training course I was asked to share briefly in a seminar at the National Portage Conference in Cambridge. Again it was exciting to attend some lectures. At one in particular there was a discussion of the new language programme which was to replace the rather inadequate language section of the checklist. In the seminar I stood in for a mother who couldn't attend. I was asked to explain how I had experienced the Portage programme as a parent.

There is always a danger in grasping hold of a system as the great solution to a problem. I explained that unless the same kind of teaching was carried out in all areas of the handicapped child's life, then the half hour of Portage work each day would not change things dramatically. However, it was very helpful and the weekly home visits were an important source of moral support.

As the child grows older and has his or her own play ideas, the Portage activities have to be slipped in unobtrusively. Elizabeth often does better if she doesn't realize that the activity matters to me. It is hard sometimes to select the most valuable activities for her to learn. She might, for instance, learn feeding and dressing by sheer practise but she was reluctant to learn to walk until she was ready herself. She would never be cajoled into it by someone else.

I worried about being critical but often psychologists work with theories and need to hear from the 'grass roots' to keep their work earthed in reality. I left, feeling apprehensive, but understood later that what I had said had been appreciated. Being allowed to be an individual with something to say at such a gathering gave me a great deal of pleasure. The conference stimulated me to go home and use the programme more effectively with Elizabeth.

A further development from the Portage programme was a link that grew with a local comprehensive school. I had offered to help the psychology department process the completed Portage charts. Then I discovered there was a possibility that they might be programmed into a school computer so that the data might be examined more carefully. It would then be possible to find out how quickly and effectively the children were learning the skills, and which were the most successful methods of teaching new activities. I was excited at the potential that such a project had. The opportunity to become involved arose through a neighbour.

The neighbour's daughter studied a child care course at the school. She chose Elizabeth for her project and eventually I was asked to speak during a lesson, taking Elizabeth with me. I was nervous as I confronted the teenagers, despite having taught the same age-group myself. But the girls were interested and were keen to hold Elizabeth. She sat happily on a science bench, enjoying the new toys and the attention. I found myself moved as I tried to explain, for the first time in public, how Elizabeth has been such a blessing to us. I hoped the visit might break down some of the prejudice that exists, based presumably on fear of the unknown. The girls could see that Elizabeth was not to be feared.

I was asked by one pupil what would happen if I had another Down's baby. I wondered if she couldn't really accept my positive attitude to Elizabeth and wanted to test out what I really felt. I admitted that it would be hard. I thought about having to go through the same process again; the early training programme, the care over diet. There would be none of the novelty and adventure that there had been with Elizabeth. Yet I knew that as God has helped us with Elizabeth, he would help us again. I admitted that I very much wanted a normal child and I didn't think that was wrong.

At the end of the talk the teacher mentioned the possibility of using the school computer, and that was how the project began. I had read several research papers about Down's syndrome. It seemed exciting to be on the very edge of something else which might be of use.

The Portage programme has helped me, not just with Elizabeth, but to become myself again. I needed something to occupy my mind. I felt guilty at having to admit that playing endless simple games with Elizabeth was sometimes very boring. To be able to use my mind in a useful way seems another avenue through which God has provided help for us during these last two years with Elizabeth.

7

Difficult Times

A few days before our holiday in Devon ended I developed cystitis. Feeling rather feeble I collected some antibiotics from a helpful health centre and felt much better by the time we had to travel home. I had suffered from cystitis before my pregnancy; during the pregnancy I couldn't believe my good fortune at being free of it. I felt discouraged now that this depressive complaint had returned. Throughout August and September I felt low and kept visiting the doctor. I found it hard to remain positive about our situation with Elizabeth.

Other people didn't always help. Well-meaning people were continually asking if Elizabeth had any teeth, why wasn't her hair growing and was she a good baby? Hair and teeth seemed irrelevant to Elizabeth's mental development. She did take a long time to cut her first tooth, Down's children often do, but I couldn't see it mattered. I hated admitting that 'Yes, she is very good.' I felt it must be because she was passive, contented and slow to see reasons for not being good. It didn't seem anything to be proud of. No doubt I was over-sensitive but sometimes I wanted to shout, 'No, she screams all day.' I thought it seemed more normal.

I realized later that Elizabeth really isn't unresponsive, nor does she sleep longer than other children. She is a happy child and there are normal children like that too. But meeting anyone exposed me afresh to facing her problems and the need to come to terms with them.

I had always believed that if I showed I was happy to talk about Elizabeth, others would feel able to do so too. This has usually been true, though a few people have totally ignored the problem. I found this difficult, but I presume it was because they couldn't face it themselves. Others denied the problem existed at all by saying that Elizabeth was getting on as well as other children of the same age. Others said, 'She will get better won't she?' or, 'She'll grow out of it.' I always tried to explain the truth to them but some didn't want to hear it.

There are other subtler forms of denial. People have said that it is all a case of what we mean by 'normal'. The problem is that what the majority of children are able to do is held as the norm by the majority of people. It is unrealistic to suggest that Down's children are normal and others are not. Someone else suggested that no child is perfect: one might have a partial hearing loss, another a squint or allergies. But there seems to me a difference between imperfections of little real consequence to one's expectations of life and something so fundamental which controls one's whole being.

46

I wonder if some people find it so hard to accept handicap because they feel inferior if they haven't had a handicapped child themselves. It is almost as if they have to pretend that they are as badly off with a normal child. But suffering is not a competition or a hierarchy with a top score for bearing the most difficult burden. I know we find it hard to come to terms with Elizabeth's problems ourselves, but having Elizabeth always with us helps us to understand and accept. It must be harder for outsiders.

At times I have felt humiliated. It was hard, across the chemist's counter, to give publicly an account of why I had a prescription for vitamins in larger doses than normal for a baby. On another occasion someone told me that I was over-protective of Elizabeth, but when other children pulled or pushed her she had little idea of looking after herself. Until she learnt to walk she was not confident of encounters with her elders, even if they were only a few inches taller than she.

There were days when I cried as I looked at her in her cot or the bath. I did think about what she could have been like. Yet I couldn't cry for long. She was there, laughing, hugging me – such a comfort. How peculiar that the cause of one's pain could also be its healer.

People were always asking to hold Elizabeth when she was small. To begin with I found this very demanding, especially when she was tiny and I was worried that she would pick up germs. One coffee morning I just couldn't take any more requests to hold her or questions about whether she was a good baby. I went home. I put Elizabeth in the pram and began to weed the garden. There were tears streaming down my face. I prodded the fork fiercely into the hard, dry ground. I wanted to be left alone. It was hard living next door to the church without even a proper fence down the side of the garden.

47

8

Towards Independence

20th September. Elizabeth's baptism
We decided to have Elizabeth baptized on the Sunday following Mark's ordination as priest at the cathedral. This meant that Mark's mother, who had kindly stayed with me while Mark was away on the pre-ordination retreat, was still with us. My parents travelled down on the evening before, so the house was full.

I looked forward to Elizabeth's baptism with expectation. I had read through the modern service a few times and felt that the words expressed what we wanted to pray for Elizabeth.

I dressed her in my baptism gown, the lace and silk slightly yellowed with time, but helping to create a sense of continuity with my own baptism and that of my sister and brother who had also worn it. On her feet I put a tiny pair of satin shoes, given to Elizabeth by a parishioner, himself the father of a handicapped son. A shawl knitted especially for the occasion and given to her by her granny, completed the dressing up. Maybe this was really the least significant part of the ceremony, but I was aware of wanting something meaningful and pretty for Elizabeth to wear. I wanted her to be the same as any other of our children, despite her handicap.

Food covered the dining-room table. There was nothing elaborate: salads, flans, cold meat and gateaux I had bought. But I had made Elizabeth a special cake and we decided to invite the vicar and his family to toast Elizabeth and share the cake before we ate our lunch.

Just before the service, Usha, a Malaysian friend, and Carolyn and Mike arrived. They were to be Elizabeth's god-parents. It was good to have a reason for seeing them again other than on our annual holiday.

I found the service a more moving experience than I had expected. The words we said came to life in a special way and Mark, himself, baptized Elizabeth. I was struck by one of the closing prayers, 'Lord God our Father . . . grant that (this child) may grow in the faith into which she has been baptized, that she may profess it for herself when she comes to be confirmed and that *all things belonging to the Spirit may live and grow in her*. Amen.'

I somehow did not doubt that Elizabeth, in her own time and way, would come to understand something about Jesus and his love for her. I had heard of other Down's children whose faith was very much their own. I felt too, that Elizabeth would be an encouragement to many people as she grew up to be part of the church family. It seemed as if 'the things belonging to the Spirit' already lived in her.

As the service ended I sensed the responsibility that lay with us to help Elizabeth understand the Christian faith, and more than that too. Through our own lives and our family life, we needed to demonstrate the reality of that faith. It was not enough to talk about it, we had to live it. How we lived would really show Elizabeth that God was at work, and that he was a loving friend intimately involved in the daily lives of his people.

After lunch, we had time to open a few of the many gifts Elizabeth had received. Two remained in my memory. Mark's mother had given her a tiny gold climbing-hut complete with pickaxe. It was intended to hang on a chain or bracelet. For me it symbolized something special. Mark's great-uncle Humphrey had been a well-known climber, who was tragically killed in a climbing accident in the Alps. His sister had also climbed, and we had known her. So there was a family significance, but also mountains, for me, symbolized the challenge of life and a mountain-hut spoke of reaching one's goal. Elizabeth might have challenges that seemed bigger for her than for other children. I felt that she would reach her goal because she belonged to God.

The other special gift was a slate paperweight, engraved by a member of our church. On the top were the letters I H S, the first three letters of the Greek word for Jesus, in lettering of the kind often found on altar cloths and pulpits.

Around the side was simply inscribed 'Elizabeth 20.9.81', and there were two fish, the early Christian symbol found engraved in the catacombs. There is a strength and simplicity about this stone that will always remind me of the simple act of faith we put into words when Elizabeth was baptized. We trusted her to God, believing that he would work in her life to bring her to know him for herself.

The day ended, as many baptisms do, with photographs for our album. It was already filled with photographs of Elizabeth from a few days old – with a tiny wrinkled face, in her cot at the hospital – to photographs showing the more rounded features of a smiling five-month-old baby. This kind of photographic record must be duplicated in millions of homes, but I suppose if someone examined our pictures more closely, they might detect something a little different about their subject.

October. Elizabeth at six months
At last we have managed to see some old college-friends again. They live in a nearby new town. Derek was a curate, also in his first job, experiencing some of the same pressures as ourselves. They had a daughter a year older than Elizabeth. They came to lunch and brought some helpful ideas. One was the babywalker they had found most useful for their daughter: a completely round one with a strong adjustable seat and a tray at the front useful for putting toys on. We had wanted to encourage Elizabeth to stand and move around. We thought this would enable her to explore and discover for herself. We had also been told that any method of encouraging stepping movements would help with walking.

We rushed off to buy the new equipment and Elizabeth was soon standing up, supported by the sling-seat and beginning to move – backwards at first – but she certainly enjoyed it. I also purchased a large piece of foam and cut out a semicircle along one side. We are trying to help Elizabeth to sit up alone and the foam seems ideal because it gives just a small support at the base of the back. If she topples over there is a soft landing. Gradually, over the last few weeks, she has balanced unsupported for longer, increasing from ten seconds to a minute by the end of the month.

Through the Portage programme we are encouraging Elizabeth to reach out her arms to be picked up. She is beginning to explore our faces when she stands on our laps. Her tiny soft fingers bring a great deal of pleasure as she gently pats and strokes. Other forms of communication are increasing too. She uses 'ma, da, ba', but also seems to imitate 'hello' when I greet her.

I sometimes feel disappointed when the only thing people seem able to say about Down's children is that they like music. But Elizabeth does listen to music, especially classical music. I understand that many normal babies and young children enjoy it, too. If Elizabeth especially enjoys it I know I should help her develop that interest, but I suppose it removes the sense of achievement if people say 'all Down's children like it'. With normal children an interest in music is admired. It seems unfair that when handicapped children appreciate it, it is spoken of as an automatic component of being handicapped. But why do I mind about all this?

November. Elizabeth at seven months

Excitement – Elizabeth sits alone for as long as ten minutes now without toppling over, so I think when people ask me if she is sitting up yet, I can say 'yes'. To prove it, Mark took a photograph of her the other day, holding onto the end of her toy telephone string. She already seems to understand that if she pulls the string the phone moves towards her.

I'm impressed by her powers of deduction. I've tried hiding some of her favourite toys under a cloth and she has begun to take the cloth off to get hold of the toys. I didn't realize how clever small babies were, nor how much they learn in a few months. At the moment even Elizabeth seems to learn a great deal.

Her interest in people is growing. She is learning to wave, and smiles and shows great interest in other children and babies. She pats and smiles at herself in the mirror too. I wonder when she will realize it is herself she is gurgling at?

I was given a place on a short Open University course

because of having a handicapped child. The subject of the course was 'The first years of life' and it has been fascinating to look at normal child development. I was especially interested in how babies of less than three months respond to a simple drawing of a face rather than to just coloured or patterned discs. Elizabeth certainly responds enthusiastically to pictures of people and animals and to cuddly toys.

She has settled into a very civilized routine now, sleeping from 7 p.m. to 7 a.m. and having her meals when we do. I still breast-feed her and she has never shown the least inclination for a bottle, so extra drinks are from a trainer-cup. She has just begun to feed herself rusks, and the beginnings of small steps towards independence excite me.

Elizabeth seems to have invented her first game. She sits on the edge of the settee, or the bed, and pushes herself off into my arms, roaring with laughter when I catch her. I can't resist playing it with her endlessly, just to hear her laugh. It really cheers me up on these dreary dull November days.

We took some photographs of Elizabeth in her baby-walker for our Christmas newsletter. She moves forward in it now, instead of sideways like a crab. She has lost the square 'Winston-Churchill-like' baby face she had, and the little heart-shaped face looking up at us above a maroon and white spotted dress and white tights seems suddenly to be that of a little girl.

December. Elizabeth at eight months

We have begun to enlarge our repertoire of nursery rhymes and action songs. I panicked when I realized I couldn't remember any right the way through and bought several books to remind myself! Elizabeth especially enjoys a rhyme about peas, with all the actions. . .

Five little peas in a pea pod pressed,
One grew, two grew and so did all the rest,
They grew and they grew and they never stopped,
Until all of a sudden the pea pod popped.

The build up to the final 'pop', with a loud clap, brings peels of laughter from her.

I have also joined the children's library on Elizabeth's behalf. She looks with interest at the large coloured picture books and although I know she can't possibly understand the stories, I enjoy reading them to her.

She is still trying hard to crawl but hasn't managed to. Sometimes she seems so very close to the pattern of normal development that I find it hard to believe she is behind. I suppose not seeing normal children develop from day to day could give me a false sense of her achievements. I am afraid of deceiving myself. Intellectually I know her handicap causes mental retardation and yet my experience day by day doesn't make me feel this. In the book *Helping your handicapped baby* there is a developmental checklist. Elizabeth is about a month behind on average, but she was three weeks early and I suppose I feel that reduces the gap. Perhaps I've still got a long way to go to real acceptance.

Elizabeth's first Christmas

All my family have arrived. It is the first time since we were married that both my brother and sister and her husband and my parents have all been together for Christmas. It is tiring, but great fun to have the house full and lots of people to talk to.

Elizabeth doesn't really understand either the excitement, the tree or the presents. She does, however, enjoy the carol services. The hymns sung in church services have always kept her quiet and interested.

When we sat down after Christmas lunch to open our presents, I popped Elizabeth onto the new wooden rocking-horse that Mark and I had given her. We had been told it would help to improve her balance. Her legs were far too short for her to begin to rock it herself, but she enjoyed pulling at the black wool mane and the white leather ears.

Elizabeth has been given so many cards and presents. I have felt overwhelmed by the generosity of many of the church family. She definitely enjoys the paper best and this always distracts her from the gift inside. But a set of plastic ducks that fit into each other are a hit for bath times. Chris gave her a wooden dog which barks when it is pulled along and that is another favourite. Many of the toys I'll put away and produce when she is bored with the ones she knows. It seems that she can only enjoy a few new things at a time; perhaps it feels safer that way.

I feel guilty that we have been given so much. The poverty that Jesus came to share that first Christmas seems a long way away from us.

January. Elizabeth at nine months

After the hectic buildup to Christmas, especially for Mark who had so many extra talks to give and services to lead, the prospect of escaping to Cornwall after the festivities were over felt like heading for an oasis of calm. Somehow we ended up travelling in the very early morning after having the church youth group's Christmas party at our home the night before. I don't really know how I managed to get organized. But we set off and arrived in Cornwall early in the afternoon.

The snow which had threatened to prevent my parents coming to stay had thawed just before Christmas, and thankfully it had not put in a second appearance. We noticed the contrast in temperature as we clambered out of the old Morris outside Mark's mother's house, stretching our cramped legs. It felt like spring here already. How beautifully green it all looked.

Granny, as she had now become, had turned a small dressing-room into a delightful bedroom for Elizabeth. The cot had belonged to the family for some time and Mark's old threadbare rabbit sat on the shelves next to it. In the corner stood a large dog on wheels, bought for Mark as a substitute for his own dog which he had insisted on tormenting by pulling its fur. Elizabeth reacted enthusiastically.

It was exciting to see her sit on the living-room floor banging her wooden xylophone that she had been given for Christmas with the stick made for that purpose. She learnt to do this in a few days and managed to draw the stick across the wooden notes to make the characteristic slide up the scale. Music must have some special attraction for her.

We bought a new wooden jigsaw with us and I was impressed that she could pick out the pieces using the tiny knobs. But Elizabeth would far rather ride in the truck my parents gave her than push it around herself.

We ended our holiday by driving across to Plymouth to see Mark's sister. After a large meal, late though it was, we decided to drive back to London to miss the traffic. It was not perhaps the wisest decision we've ever made!

The Morris broke down. Elizabeth slept in her carry-cot but I felt anxious in the cold night air as we lugged her into a service station restaurant and waited for help to come. It was 2 a.m. when we finally set off for London. We were both feeling bleary-eyed and as if it was all a dream. The indoor plants in a large brick trough in the restaurant stayed in my mind for weeks afterwards. I must have stared at them, half asleep, for a long time.

Thankfully, Elizabeth didn't seem to mind and only occasionally stirred. The seemingly interminable journey over, and Elizabeth settled in her cot, we clambered into bed, sleeping gratefully, if very briefly, before the day began again. We vowed we would never take a small baby on that kind of midnight madness again. Secretly I longed for a newer car!

February. Elizabeth at ten months

Elizabeth seems to have made more progress again this month. Her ability to communicate is developing. She says 'ted, ted' when given her teddy. I suppose it is her second word if 'dada' is included too. When I ask where owl's eyes are she touches the brown felt discs of the woolly owl that Granny gave her for Christmas. She turns to us when we call her name and begins to move towards us in her baby-walker. Her ability to understand is growing encouragingly.

Physically, too, she is progressing. She can move around on her tummy and walks a few steps when holding on to the back of the baby-walker. She is even beginning to dance to music if we hold her hands.

Elizabeth continues to show a great interest in pictures and tries to pick up the objects. But her interest does not just lie with what the pictures show. A great treat is to be given a piece of greaseproof paper which she likes to crumple for a long time before finally attempting to eat it.

Her selection of favourite toys has increased. Toys that roll and move across the floor, and toys that can be banged or rattled are popular. She likes the little egg-men that never fall over when they are pushed, and a simple car with a large man that fits into a hole in the centre. I am surprised that she has no problems in understanding representations of people; anything with two eyes interests her. She has discovered the delight of knocking down towers that are painstakingly built for her, and taking objects out of boxes.

I would like to relax and not worry about what Elizabeth is learning, yet sometimes I feel as if it takes such a long time for her to grasp something. I have spent ages showing her how to put the man into the hole in the car, but she finds it hard to do. I expect I am too impatient. Neither is it any good expecting her to achieve something she isn't yet capable of. When I look back through my diary it is encouraging to see her progress, but day by day I get frustrated. Perhaps I am trying to make her keep up with the activities I know fit her age. I have got to learn to accept that she won't be able to do so.

March. Elizabeth at eleven months

I decided to take Elizabeth on the train to see Mark's mother for a few days. I felt I needed a change. I am tired and sometimes find it hard to cope with the stream of people that come to the door.

Mark drove us to Paddington and I managed to put all we needed into two soft zip-bags. I had the buggy and a tie-on seat that would act as Elizabeth's high chair. It was a flat piece of material designed to slot over a chair back and to tie round the baby's tummy. I felt pleased with my rare economy on luggage.

Fortunately, the train was not crowded and we found two empty seats opposite a pleasant-looking woman reading a newspaper. I sat Elizabeth by the window with a few toys and books. To begin with, at least, she was happy to look round the carriage and at the fields and houses as we sped by. She had never been on a train before.

Several times I could see her trying to make contact with the lady opposite. She kept smiling at her every time the paper was lowered. But there was no response. I felt sad that someone was unable to react to such a small person who was trying so hard to be friendly. Perhaps she hadn't known many babies.

Eventually, Elizabeth fell asleep on my lap and apart from the problem of trying to change her nappy on the bouncing railway seat, the rest of the journey was peaceful. By the time we reached our destination my arm was numb with Elizabeth's weight, but I was delighted that she had been so good, and I was pleased to see Mark's mother waiting on the platform.

Elizabeth soon felt at home as she rushed around the wide corridors and across the slate kitchen-floor in her baby-walker. Her feet were clad in her very first pair of leather shoes, not because she could walk, but to stop her tights sliding on the floors. Elizabeth seemed more confident about the dogs than on our last visit and babbled away to them happily.

I had been encouraged by friends in the Down's group to introduce Elizabeth to a potty. I was told it was important to establish habits early. I was not quite convinced as I'd always felt one should leave potties until after two years old, when the child was really ready. But I thought there wasn't much to lose. I would forget it if she rebelled later on. She seemed to have no problem understanding its purpose and I proudly showed her granny how happily she sat on it. Despite my misgivings I couldn't hide my pleasure in this seeming step forward.

On the second day we spent in Cornwall I was excited to discover how quickly Elizabeth could learn something. She had been touching my eyes, nose and mouth when I asked her where each was, so I decided to teach her the word 'hair'. I realized later to my cost that perhaps an ear would have been better! After two demonstrations – my placing her hand on my hair and saying the word – she touched it herself when I asked. The ability to communicate with a small child continues to amaze and delight me. Whether it is because Elizabeth is handicapped or not, I am always surprised at what she understands. Each new word feels like a breakthrough.

The only thing that marred our stay in Cornwall was the throat infection Elizabeth developed. It is only the second infection she has had so I know we are very fortunate, but nevertheless I still felt anxious on the day her temperature was highest. She slept a great deal and made a complete recovery in three or four days. The penicillin had worked well and I was encouraged by her apparent resistance to illness which must have aided the rapid recovery. The previous infection had taken longer to disappear, but inexperience had made me think she would get better and I had not taken her to the doctor sufficiently early. This time we took no risks and I felt more confident about her health as a result.

10th April. Elizabeth at one year

It seems so much longer than a year since Elizabeth was born. I suppose more has happened to us in this time than in any other single year of our lives.

We were invited to a reunion with friends from university and it seemed an appropriate way to celebrate Elizabeth's birthday. All our friends had babies and one of these was my god-daughter. It would also be the last time for a few years that we would see one of the couples, a doctor and his wife, and their small son whom we hadn't yet met. They were leaving England to work in a mission hospital in Kenya.

The drive through the Buckinghamshire countryside to our friends' house, not far from where I'd spent my teenage years, was really enjoyable. We still get such a hemmed-in feeling, living where we do. The lack of hills and open spaces presses in on us and even the windows of our Victorian house do not look out onto the garden. So we were grateful for this sense of space and the warmth of the Easter sun shining through the car windows.

Apart from the delicious meal, it was fun to meet again and to see the children, each one a unique expression of people we had known very well. I produced a birthday cake and held Elizabeth up to blow out the candle. She needed some assistance, but enjoyed the fun.

I noticed how mobile my god-daughter was. She is a month older than Elizabeth, but much larger, crawling between table-legs and pulling herself up on the furniture. She is a beautiful child, but I didn't feel sad about Elizabeth.

I would have liked her hair to grow and her cheeks not to be so red, but she had a special quality of her own which I felt proud of. I felt proud, too, of her own attempts to crawl even though she only pulls herself along by her arms. At least she is moving about on her own now.

I'm glad it wasn't painful to see this normal child alongside my own. In many ways they still seem close in age. They shared the same baked fish and potato lunch, and home-made yoghurt for pudding, in the same high chair. My god-daughter did seem to have more idea of what spoons were for, but I know one day Elizabeth will feed herself. They are both too young to do so now.

We drove home again, enjoying the sense of freedom, but earlier than we would have wished. The next day was Easter Sunday and Mark had a sermon to finish. I had a long session playing records to Elizabeth, singing and beating her xylophone and a drum which we had borrowed from the toy library at the school for handicapped children. Elizabeth had clearly enjoyed her first birthday.

9

Healing?

The telephone rang one morning. It was a parishioner. Elizabeth was about four months old at the time. The woman at the other end of the phone was excited. She had just heard a report on the radio about some new research into vitamins. The research had been carried out in the USA and the results suggested that mentally-handicapped children could be helped by large doses of vitamins and minerals. I hurriedly sent off for the information sheet which included the name of the journal where we could find the report of the research. Mark happened to be going to Nottingham on a short course and was able to obtain a copy of the article from the university library. We read it with interest.

The astounding claim was that in some cases the children,

treated with a six-month course of various vitamins and minerals in very large doses, had reached an IQ level 25 points above their previous level. Could this be the answer for Elizabeth? I sent a copy of the article to her paediatrician, impatiently waiting for a reply.

The paediatrician was guarded in her response. Apparently only two of the children in the trial had Down's syndrome. It was not clear whether the children lived in institutions. If they did, then the poor diet, followed by extra vitamins, could account for such an increase in IQ. She warned us not to raise our hopes falsely, but said she would willingly discuss the matter with us.

I had wanted her to tell us that this was the answer; the way out. I felt disappointed but I knew, too, the wisdom of her reply. She didn't want us to rush after all the miracle cures we heard of, to be more disappointed than ever when they failed to solve the problem.

There was other research being done into Down's syndrome. In France, Lejeune was working on metabolism. He thought that there might be results in about ten years' time, which might help to treat the symptoms of Down's syndrome. No one could rectify the cause. The Down's Children's Association had already issued an information sheet on safe doses of vitamins and other aspects of diet which had been found to help Down's children. Neither of these sources provided the rapid results of the American research. I should have realized that it takes a long time to obtain reliable results. I still needed to accept the slow pathway that lay ahead of teaching Elizabeth day by day, being careful about her diet, and also praying that each day we could do things that would help her to fulfil her potential.

We did talk to the paediatrician and decided on acceptable doses of vitamin E, ABIDEC (a multi-vitamin preparation) and iron. Gradually I read more about vitamin research and added small doses of vitamin C and B6 to the list. The paediatrician was in agreement with this.

At a branch meeting of the Down's Children's Association, a London doctor spoke about his own project to test the validity of the American claims. He believed that overdoses of all vitamins could be dangerous. He was worried that parents were beginning to experiment independently of medical advice, and he wanted to help them to find out the truth. Vitamins on prescription would cost the Health Service a great deal and this money could be better spent elsewhere if it was shown that vitamins made no difference to our children's development.

It was possible that vitamin deficiency and its results could help solve the huge problems facing the Health Service in dealing with senile dementia and other geriatric disorders. Thus perhaps the limited area of research into handicap could have far wider implications. Down's people age more rapidly than others and senile dementia occurs earlier than in the general population. Could vitamin therapy affect this problem?

I left the meeting convinced of the need to be careful of vitamin dosage but still feeling that safe doses of vitamins could help. Elizabeth had always been very healthy. Although we couldn't prove that vitamins had helped, it was hard to deny the possibility. If she had more days when she was well and was able to learn new things, her mental development would be helped too. Even if this was the only result, it seemed sensible to continue. I thought, too, about developing countries where brain damage has been shown to occur in malnourished children. If Down's children can compensate for their faulty absorption of vitamins by taking slightly larger doses, then their brains as well as their bodies might be helped to grow healthily.

When confronted with an insurmountable problem, we tend to look for dramatic or easy ways out. When Elizabeth was born, several friends mentioned the possibility of praying for God to heal her. I had experienced something of God's healing power for myself on two or three previous occasions. It had not been dramatic, but I felt certain that God was at work in a special way because people had prayed and laid hands on me. But when I thought about Elizabeth I couldn't see how it could be appropriate. She was permanently handicapped. To ask for healing would mean asking God to change the fundamental structure of each cell in her body.

When she was very small I pushed the idea to the back of my mind. To start with it seemed to confuse my sense of

God planning Elizabeth for us. Later, I tried to think about what healing meant for Elizabeth. I wondered if part of our answer was that God was at work for her good through the vitamins and the stimulation programme. Then about a year afterwards an Indian Christian was invited to our church to take a healing service. He had been used by God to pray for many sick people who had been subsequently healed of cancer and other incurable diseases. I felt that we should take Elizabeth to the service and ask him to pray for her. It seemed wrong to neglect this opportunity for help that was on our doorstep.

The service was encouraging and at the end, when the preacher gently placed his hands on Elizabeth's head and prayed for her, I felt that God was at work. We did not see dramatic changes, but the winter that followed the service was a very healthy one for Elizabeth. I don't feel that we can tell God what to do nor how to answer our prayers. I believe that as we continue to pray for Elizabeth God will continue to work out his plan for her. Having Elizabeth prayed for on specific occasions is a way of affirming that we depend entirely on God for her well-being and that we need his power in our lives. He may choose to work through human means or other means, but we have always felt he has worked for good in her life.

A question we have to ask, and not just for Elizabeth, is what does health and healing mean? We cannot really say that increasing Elizabeth's IQ by 25 points is all or indeed even a part of healing. Health affects our minds and bodies and the spiritual part of us too. To live a healthy life includes our relationships with others and what we are able to give because of the well-being within us. Perhaps in her own way Elizabeth could be healthier than many of us. Yet we also want the best for her. We want her to have a chance to learn and to develop some independence. But even independence can be a goal we exaggerate in importance. We all need others.

At a purely practical level it was interesting to watch a television programme showing how plastic surgery had been used on some Down's children to shorten their tongues, to improve their speech, and to adjust the slant of their eyes.

People asked me if we would have Elizabeth treated in this way. Apparently many of the children who had undergone surgery gained in confidence as a result. But the fact that their handicap was no longer observable, to the casual passer-by, meant that they could become more vulnerable to abuse and ill-treatment. Elizabeth is too young yet for such a venture, but it is worth considering the issues involved.

Ten or twenty years ago research into vitamins and plastic surgery for Down's children were not thought of. I can only be grateful that such possibilities are available today. We trust that God will guide us to the right answers as part of his answer to our prayers for Elizabeth's well-being. I find it easier to accept now that it is unlikely she will be cured or transformed overnight. Sometimes it is hard to visualize her being different – perhaps we don't really wish it, because we love her for who she is. We feel sure that as we continue to put her in God's hands he will work in her the health that she needs.

THE
SECOND
YEAR

10

A Way Forward

May. Elizabeth at thirteen months

At the end of last month I stopped breast-feeding Elizabeth. I felt sad on the last occasion. We would no longer share this very intimate form of communication. I remembered times when she had been a tiny baby, so responsive as she had held her hands around a breast and sucked hard. Now it was no longer a very serious business for her. Seeing my reactions when she clamped her two teeth hard onto my nipple seemed like fun to her, so I felt it was time to stop.

My sadness might have been linked as well to a fear that I would never do it again. Until I actually held another child in my arms, I could not be confident that it would happen. But I was surprised, as the days passed, that neither of us seemed to miss it as much as I'd feared. Occasionally Elizabeth asked for a feed again, but was easily distracted. I'd been most concerned about early mornings, but found that once she was up and ready for breakfast there were no problems. As for myself, the newfound freedom to wear what I wanted and the fact that I was not so tired were an unexpected bonus.

The only reaction that has marred this move towards independence is Elizabeth's refusal to drink anything from a cup. She had been quite proficient when she was still breast-fed. I had foolish visions of dehydration and kidney damage, not helped by a friend's comments. But another, more experienced, mother reassured me that her son had stopped drinking entirely for a month after she stopped feeding him. I was impressed that such young children could voice their protests so strongly and was encouraged that Elizabeth was demonstrating her feelings in such a normal way.

Somehow, I feel as if Elizabeth is no longer making as much progress as she has done. She has learnt to pull the cord on her musical box to entertain herself in the early mornings. The first time it happened I was sure that Mark must have gone in to her room to turn it on, and then I saw him asleep next to me. That was quite an exciting moment! She walks around holding onto only one of our hands now, but is very unsteady on her feet. She enjoys her books and turns the pages to look at the pictures. But the thing I find most difficult to cope with is her lack of concentration. She gets bored so easily with everything. We think of new activities to try with the Portage programme, but she soon refuses to co-operate.

A milestone, usually reached at around a year, is the ability to give objects to people and to put them in boxes. We have been encouraging Elizabeth to do this for what seems like months, but she still is not able to. I suppose because it seems an important goal to us, it feels the more unattainable when she doesn't reach it. I wish it didn't matter so much. No doubt it matters simply because I so desperately want her to keep up or at least to be only a month or so behind.

I was delighted when I managed to encourage her to give me some toys herself. I hid them in my hands for her to find. She enjoyed guessing which hand they were in and getting them back herself, and then she enthusiastically returned the objects for another game. But even that didn't last for many days. It seems that the point of the activity has to be very clear to Elizabeth otherwise she will not participate.

My sense of disappointment increased when I read in *Helping your handicapped baby* about levels of play at different ages. The level Elizabeth seems to be operating at, at present, is 'a tool user', the seven to ten months level.

We started a weekly mums and toddlers Bible-study group last January. The children who come with their mothers are slightly younger than Elizabeth. Each week I see their progress and gradually they have begun to catch up with Elizabeth. I suppose this has added to my current sense of despondency.

I noticed recently how a small eight-month-old was trying to place a ring onto a pyramid. It looked so easy to her. I have been practising this with Elizabeth for several months and she still cannot do it. It suddenly seemed so unfair. Other children appeared to learn effortlessly while we had to work patiently week by week and hope she understood. Being reminded weekly of the slowness of her progress didn't help.

Yet I know I must accept that Elizabeth is behind and will be behind. Until now, she has seemed so close to normal that I have been lulled into a false appreciation of her ability. Why am I obsessed with the level of her progress? We are supposed to be learning to value Elizabeth for herself, not for what she can do. I seem to be failing dismally. Perhaps it takes much longer than a year to dismantle the edifices built in thirty.

I think there is another aspect to this struggle. When Elizabeth was born, we were told it would be impossible to predict her ability and we would have to take each day as it came. There is quite a wide range in the ability of Down's children, from an IQ score as low as 30 or 40 to over 70. (IQ measurements are of limited value in giving a true picture of a child but nevertheless are the kind of tool used in comparisons.)

By trying to gauge Elizabeth's level of development now I suppose I am trying to cope with my uncertainty about the future. Yet all the time I know how complex it is. Experts speak about possible plateaux of development at age seven, and yet also that Down's children continue to learn well into their twenties and thirties if they continue to be taught. Their development takes longer than normal and may not follow a steady progression.

I had been led to believe that there could be a fall-off in Elizabeth's development. She would seem close to normal as a baby and then the gap would widen. I feel frightened about how big the gap will be and how suddenly it will widen. Each time, therefore, that Elizabeth reaches a milestone, I breath a sigh of relief and think 'it hasn't happened yet'. When she doesn't reach these goals the future seems to stretch before us with her never walking or talking, but sitting in a corner mute and placid. Yet now she isn't mute and placid, and I find it hard, in more rational moments, to believe that the continued stimulation will not in some way give her a foundation for her development and learning. I suppose it depends on how hopeful I'm feeling.

There is another unknown that even the experts cannot predict. It is only very recently, within maybe the last ten years, that people have seriously tried to teach Down's children more and have believed that they could learn more. The Portage programme was only recently introduced to Britain. The methods of using early stimulation, advocated by Rex Brinkworth and the Down's Children's Association, have also only been practised for a relatively short time.

We will not be able to see the effects of this early training and learning until the new generation of Down's children has grown older. A few are attending normal schools for varying periods of time, and more attend ESN (mild) schools (for children with IQ 50–70).

All we know is that through this century the average IQ score for Down's children has risen from 29 before the war to 50–60 today for children who have had stimulation from birth. (Figures from Rex Brinkworth, 1982, Down's Children's Association.) Their ability to learn and to live more independently has improved remarkably with the right kind of help.

So I suppose that wanting Elizabeth to continue to progress is part of trying to build up a realistic picture of her for the future. It is part of a human need for predictability and security, but I need to move beyond that and to enjoy Elizabeth day by day and simply to trust God for the outcome.

I find this trusting attitude is harder to maintain after

visits from one particular friend and her child. Perhaps she finds it hard to imagine how I feel. She usually begins her visit by telling me all the new things her child has learnt. The child is almost the same age as Elizabeth, and extremely intelligent. Eventually, she might ask me what Elizabeth is doing and I reply rather weakly with something her child has obviously learnt long ago. Invariably after she has left with her child, I pick Elizabeth up and cry. Not because Elizabeth can't do the same activities, but because I feel hurt and misunderstood. Elizabeth's limitations feel just part of the furniture, not something to be concerned about or to share in. It is then that I feel isolated and alone.

I used to cope with this isolation by buying toys and books. Magazines told us these toys would help our child. I bought anything that I felt would stimulate Elizabeth. I felt guilty about buying so much, yet it made me feel better. I wonder if I thought that buying a particular toy would magically enable her to achieve the new skill. That was the way I had thought about books when I was younger; almost believing that once the book was bought the knowledge was automatically assimilated. I forgot that the book had to be read and digested slowly.

Yet the toy-buying made me feel like other mothers. It broke down the isolation. It was something I could share in. I bought books about how to be a gifted parent, how to teach your baby to read and to swim, as well as books on handicap. I thought I might find ways to help Elizabeth but perhaps I did it for myself as well.

Now I can see that all this was a way of coping with, and perhaps of not really accepting, the problem of Elizabeth's handicap. I feel as if the only real way to cope is to enjoy Elizabeth for herself and to accept her limitations without minding. There is a great deal about her to enjoy. She is fascinated by the sieve inside a fish that can be taken apart, and it is thrilling to see her inspect this object minutely in the bath and try to work out how it operates. She enjoys the spinning-top humming on the carpet and is beginning to learn how to make it spin. Her interest in pictures is growing and she is learning to point to different ones. She is beginning to pull herself up to stand, too. I long just to relax and enjoy her for herself without comparison.

She eats and sleeps a lot at the moment and is growing quickly. I wonder if she is developing so much physically that she has no extra energy for the activities I think she should accomplish.

I wish I didn't get bored with trying to play with her. Sometimes I find it hard to think of new ideas. I have begun to see how easy it would be to be completely obsessed by one's child. I fear already that I focus too much of my attention on Elizabeth.

I know that having another child would help me to keep things in perspective and yet I feel that Elizabeth needs the time on her own first to learn as much as she can. I am in a cleft stick. It is a real struggle to wait, yet I feel that I have to. I know I worry too much about the amount of time I put in to playing with Elizabeth and feel so much depends on myself, but it seems impossible to risk not teaching her, in case she doesn't learn anything on her own.

I know God is the only one who can sort out the muddle I seem to be in. I have tried to hand over these feelings and frustrations to God this month and I have found two areas of practical help have arrived.

Reading the section in *Helping your handicapped baby* on the development of the child from one to two years, I was reassured to discover that each child, as he passes one year, begins to develop his own individuality. His interests widen and he may concentrate on one aspect of development and then another. It is harder to get a child to comply with adult requests because he is now establishing his own ideas and preferences. The best way to help him to play is to let him choose activities himself and then to draw alongside and extend his play ideas and skills. I was relieved to see how Elizabeth fits closely into this pattern and that there is a way forward.

The second area of help came from becoming part of a private tutoring organization. I visit two families for an hour a week to help with extra reading. At the moment I can take Elizabeth with me. I hope later to have an older pupil to coach for exams. I feel excited about this new area of interest.

It widens my vision and prevents me from being obsessed with trying to make Elizabeth do things she is neither ready nor willing to try. It helps to keep things in perspective.

I have just begun to process the charts for the Portage project, and I enjoy the challenge because the work is complicated. I hope that it will contribute to research into the value of Portage. I am grateful to have these opportunities to use skills that are part of myself, but lie dormant because of the everyday practicalities of life with a small baby. I feel that what is happening is part of the process of finding myself again after all that has happened to change our lives. It is good to see that God is with us, especially in the times when we feel at the end of our own resources, providing encouragement and a way forward.

June. Elizabeth at fourteen months

Our second holiday with Carolyn and Mike made me realize how much of a strain we must have been under last year. We have been able to relax so much more. The weather hasn't been good, but there is plenty to do and Elizabeth has enjoyed it.

We went to the West Country after a friend's wedding in Brighton at which Mark was an usher. Elizabeth wore a red and white dress with the words 'Have a nice day' embroidered on the pocket. She looked rather sweet and was well behaved considering the stifling heat at the reception. We drove on to Bodmin after a night with college friends, and spent the first week with Mark's mother.

Elizabeth was again fascinated by the dogs which loved to mill around her high chair at mealtimes. She spent a long time chatting to them, holding out sticky marmite fingers to their hairy faces and delighting in their dogginess. She saw cows, ducks and pigs for the first time and liked them too.

One hot golden morning we went to the beach, where Elizabeth investigated the sand. She ate huge quantities and showed only a passing interest in the large beach-ball and Daddy filling buckets with sand. It will be another year before we can fulfil our desires to demonstrate our skills at building sand-castles. The memory of a small figure in a white frilly sun-hat and blue swim-suit, trying to eat seaweed, will remain with me.

We used Mark's father's cine camera to film Elizabeth's attempts to walk. We found the most successful method was to place a rolled-up sheet under her armpits and then to let her toddle around while we held the ends. She must have looked peculiar to others, but she enjoyed it immensely.

In Devon we spent several afternoons with Elizabeth wading out to sea, supported by her sheet. She loved the waves despite their coldness.

I enjoyed seeing Carolyn and Mike's new daughter, also called Elizabeth. She is remarkably advanced physically and learnt to crawl while we were on holiday. At six months, I was impressed. I did reflect that in fact she crawled better than our Elizabeth does now, as she is still pulling herself around on her elbows, but it was a delight to see such an active and beautiful baby.

Our evenings were spent watching a run of good films on television and sampling the culinary expertise of our husbands who always treated us to a few nights off while we were on holiday. And long games of Scrabble and Monopoly, large jigsaws and books, filled any spare time we had.

I managed to have a long talk to Carolyn one evening which began as we bathed the children together. I shared some of the muddle I had felt about wanting another child.

For the first time I admitted that it is neither wrong nor unnatural to want another, normal child. It is strange how quick I have been to feel that what I want cannot be what God wants for me. In fact, God has had to show me on several occasions that he wants the very best for us; often a far better thing than we can imagine. Sometimes he has given me something, or someone, and it has only been after the event that I have understood how much I wanted that very thing and had never before realized it. Psalm 37 says, 'Delight yourself in God and he will give you the desires of your heart.'

God loves to give; he has given us a world to enjoy. He is the great giver and creator. Yet sometimes I hardly dare to believe it. I know that he will not hold back what is truly good and right for us, yet perhaps, because I know how much I want another baby, I fear the power of my wanting.

Voicing my desire made me feel suddenly very excited. Discussing the practicalities of how it would fit in with a probable move next summer made it feel like a real possibility. The possibility of becoming pregnant next spring seemed so much more bearable than waiting until Elizabeth was three, the self-imposed time-scale I had held up as the ideal for Elizabeth. A weight fell from my mind.

I'd been concerned to accept Elizabeth completely. I did not want a substitute child. But maybe I had been hard on myself about how much one is able to accept at any one time.

I was pleased to read that Down's children seemed to benefit as much from the stimulation of young brothers and sisters as from the undivided attention of a parent. The weight of responsibility dropped away further. I knew another child would help us see Elizabeth in perspective, as a part of our family rather than the focus of it. It couldn't be helpful for her or for me if I was obsessed with her progress and focussed all my efforts upon her unhealthily. The more I thought, the more relieved I became.

We returned home from our holiday feeling we had really relaxed and were more able to face the demands of the parish again. I shall always remember the way Elizabeth greeted everyone each morning when we piled into the Devon farmhouse kitchen for breakfast, her hand held out to be kissed, like a queen. She certainly had enjoyed herself too.

September. Elizabeth at seventeen months
We have just returned from a week's holiday with my parents in their 300-year-old Cotswold cottage. It was a happy week. Elizabeth made her first visit to a bird sanctuary. Once she had become accustomed to peering through the wire netting she responded very positively to the birds, especially the penguins. But perhaps the most exciting part of the holiday for us was the feeling we both had that the period of stagnation in Elizabeth's development is over. She suddenly seems to have understood many of the skills we have been teaching her for several months.

We were sitting on the thick green patterned carpet in the living room of the cottage when Elizabeth started to put a peg-man into its narrow hole in her 'pop-up men' toy. Now she is putting her nesting beakers one inside the other and posting bricks into her post-box. She loves the 'Holly Hobby' set of tins I borrowed from the Pram Club and piles them on top of each other. She has also learnt to put rings onto the spindle to make a pyramid.

Perhaps the last few months haven't been wasted after all. Children's development tends to occur in what appears outwardly to be 'fits and starts'. They seem to grasp many things simultaneously and then have a period of consolidation. This plateau and step type of development seems to be more obvious in Down's children. Perhaps it is because their learning is slower than others. There is also another aspect to the seeming stagnation. I read, in a research paper, a study of several Down's children's development over a period of five years or so. It revealed that a slowing down of development occurred between ten and sixteen months. Elizabeth has fitted into this pattern to some extent. Perhaps this is another aspect of the little-understood complexities of Down's syndrome. We are relieved anyway that progress seems to be starting again.

Elizabeth is also beginning to extend her eating habits. She used to restrict herself to bananas, yoghurt and ryvita, marmite and a mince and vegetable dinner; healthy food, if rather limited. But to my surprise, a few weeks ago she sat on a friend's carpet and ate a whole apple, and I discovered she likes grapes and cherries too. One day recently we walked to the park to look at the ducks and ended up sitting on a bench sharing a bag of cherries between us. I have tried hard to restrict Elizabeth's carbohydrate intake as I have always been anxious about her becoming overweight, but she still shows little interest in eating bread so I don't think I need to worry at the moment. Unfortunately, her eating habits have also extended to spiders and flies, but I'm not convinced that she enjoyed these delicacies very much.

Each day we have a routine which seems to suit Elizabeth. She usually wakes up at 6.40 a.m. and sings and talks in her cot until she gets up. After breakfast I like to spend the time before her morning sleep playing with her and doing the Portage activities. She is beginning to play quite imaginatively with dolls, giving them cuddles, feeding them with bottles and sometimes even calling them 'baby' or her equivalent. She says 'Mumma, Dadda, Tedda and duck' too, but with varied regularity.

Her interest in books is extending. In July I was delighted when she began to point to the cat and the brush in her large 'talkabout' book when asked where these pictures were. Now she can point to other pictures too. It seems clear that her understanding of pictures is more advanced than that of objects at the moment. Research suggests that Down's children understand visual images better than three-dimensional ones. Elizabeth certainly seems to fall into this pattern.

Certain books are great favourites, especially those featuring cats and other animals. Elizabeth is showing her own preferences for all kinds of things more clearly day by day.

After Elizabeth has slept and had her lunch we usually go out shopping, to friends or to the Pram Club where she enjoys meeting other children. She sees normal children almost every day and I am pleased that she has this stimulation. We try to be home for five o'clock when Mark comes in. He usually plays with Elizabeth while I get an early meal. She enjoys these times especially. Bathtimes follow supper. These are times to experiment with flannels that absorb water and are fun to suck and ducks that sometimes float and pots that fill with water.

Bathtime usually ends with a struggle to get Elizabeth dressed. She dislikes this part of the routine most of all. She is happiest if she can crawl quickly away from me, nappy in hand, roaring with laughter. The potty-training I was so proud of a few months ago has been clearly and definitely discontinued by Elizabeth. She refuses to sit on the potty, but then laughs as she stands up and performs on the floor. I am convinced she understands all about this particular idea, but has decided it is one area that she will have control of. I am waiting patiently!

Discipline is something we feel confused about at the moment. As far as potty-training is concerned I feel Elizabeth isn't ready. But she pulls hair and does understand the meaning of 'no'. She also tears wallpaper off the bathroom wall. I am loathe to smack her for fear of her imitative skills making the situation worse. She is too young to understand reasoning so ignoring bad behaviour and rewarding good still seems to be the best policy. It happens, too, to be that advocated by the Portage programme. Nevertheless, sometimes I am afraid we are not as firm as we need to be. Elizabeth needs to know clearly what is allowed and what is not.

At least going to bed is not an event that Elizabeth wants to protest about. After we have prayed very simply about the day and waved 'night night', Elizabeth happily settles down to sleep, pushing the soft dome on her activity centre and sucking her mouth. She rarely wakes up until the next morning.

Life feels more hopeful and stable now. I know, too, that my more positive feelings relate to the other exciting development of this month. We decided not to wait until next spring. I am sure I am pregnant.

11

Fear of Rejection

During the first year after Elizabeth's birth a news scandal blew up which affected me more deeply than most other events reported. It was the beginning of a series of programmes and reports relating to Down's syndrome, which left me feeling hurt and angry. It seemed that those who spoke most loudly and insistently were those who had only negative views to proclaim. The 'Doctor Arthur Case', as it became known, involved a Down's baby born in Derby. He was rejected by his parents on the day of his birth and allowed to die by being given drugs which suppressed his appetite. The coroner's report confirmed a serious heart defect and possible gut problems. There followed a court case between representatives of a group called 'Life' and the doctor and social services concerned. The doctor was accused of murder but found not guilty.

Much discussion of handicap followed, including interviews on radio which painted a very depressing and dated picture of the sort of life a Down's child could expect to lead. Much was said to support the termination of the Derbyshire baby's life.

A correpsondence in *The Church Times* continued the debate with a letter I found disturbing. Someone, who did not state his own involvement with handicapped people, spoke about the burden a sixteen-year-old Down's boy would be to his parents, with unfulfilled sexual desires and the need to be kept occupied. He criticized 'do-gooders' who spoke positively about such children and said that they should spend their holidays looking after them before making such comments.

In fact, Down's boys are generally thought to have a low sexual drive and there seem to be many activities which they can happily enjoy at all ages.

The debate was taken up on television. One film showed a twenty-year-old Down's girl being taken to the park with her mother. She walked along a wall and jumped off, like many small children would. She was dressed in ankle socks and a child's-style dress, despite being of adult build. The mother was interviewed and said that she wished her child had never lived.

This was followed by an interview with Rex Brinkworth and his sixteen-year-old daughter, Francoise. Rex Brinkworth plays a leading role in the Down's Children's Association, founded in 1970. Francoise had been born with very poor muscle tone. Her father had worked hard to stimulate her with exercises and diet, despite feeling that her potential was unlikely to be great. She was filmed having a piano lesson, then asked some questions. 'Do you know what is wrong with you?'

'Yes, I have 47 chromosones; in the world they have 46.'

'Do you know what this illness is called?'

'No.'

She was an attractive, dark-haired girl, dressed prettily. She was learning French and said she would like to be a waitress when she left school. It appeared that her life was filled with activities appropriate to her age and ability. The contrast with the previous film was striking.

Later that year – the Year of Disabled People – a documentary was shown called *Kathy Leaves Home*. A seventeen-year-old Down's girl was leaving home to begin life in a community for handicapped people. The programme described her family life with her four brothers and sisters, and with her parents who were house-parents in a boys' boarding-school. This was followed by an account of the applications, interviews and the eventual offer to Kathy of a place in the community. She visited the community daily for a few weeks, gradually finding her own role there and making friends. She was taken to choose curtains, carpet and furniture for her bedroom which she was to share with another handicapped girl. The staff stressed the importance of each member making choices, having a role to play and finding work which suited their ability and interests within the large house and garden.

Then the day arrived for Kathy to move in. She was seen waving from the steps as her parents drove away. It was hard not to cry as I imagined the emotions of a mother leaving her daughter behind to belong somewhere else; leaving someone so vulnerable. But the enthusiasm of the staff was obvious and their vision of each person as an individual who really mattered, excited me.

Kathy's mother never seemed to be quite at home with her daughter. She had been sent to boarding-school at the age of five. At the time she needed to be strapped into a high chair to eat her meals. Very soon after arriving at the school she was eating her meals normally at the table with the other children. At home now with her family she appeared to be a very polite, helpful teenager, but her mother spoke about the anxiety that filled each day. It was obvious that her mother felt if Kathy had not been given a place in the community their family life would have been in jeopardy. She felt it would be impossible for her husband to continue as house-master if Kathy lived at home with them. Viewing her life with Kathy, her mother admitted that if an amniocentisis and abortion had been offered to her in pregnancy, she would have accepted both. The programme ended there.

Another documentary screened was about a Down's boy in his twenties, brought up at home. A trailer showed his mother saying how his life deteriorated daily, with nothing for him to do at home. 'People like him should never have been born' she said.

I began to feel overwhelmed by the negativity of it all. The overall impression given by the media was that handicapped children were simply a burden to society and to their parents, and it would be better if they never lived. Nowhere could I see or hear parents speaking of what their handicapped child gave to them. Was I being naïvely optimistic about Elizabeth? The joy I experienced in knowing her was very real, yet no one seemed to be prepared to speak in public about this. After watching these programmes I found myself compelled to go and look at Elizabeth, asleep in her cot. Perhaps it was to reassure myself of how much I loved her and, too, of how lovable she is. I cried with relief on many occasions and sometimes picked her up, still warmly asleep and relaxed, to hug her. I felt strengthened then in my resolve to stand against the negativity and rejection.

These programmes and a book I subsequently read raised many questions. The Doctor Arthur case made me think about the way parents are told of their child's handicap. I wondered if there had been no question of terminating the baby's life on the first day, whether things might have been different. The parents must have been deeply shocked and upset and there had been no chance for a bond to grow between mother and child. If the doctors had waited a few days the child's life might have been saved.

One family that we were introduced to had a Down's child as their first baby. The mother had initially rejected the baby, but her husband had taken her day by day to the hospital to feed him. After ten days the mother said, 'We can't leave him here, let's take him home.' He is now a happy and loved member of the family with a younger brother and sister.

A friend of mine told me how she had wanted to smother her baby when she first heard of his handicap. But this feeling disappeared rapidly and in its place came a love and acceptance which I admire.

Perhaps if the Derbyshire parents had been given more time and had not been offered the option of euthanasia there would not have been the irreversible result of the baby's death. It seems strange that the possible option of death should be offered to parents. If the child had been normal, even with the physical problems he had, this would never have occurred. It seems in this case as if the child's handicap made him of no value. He was treated as less than human. It was inconvenient and expensive to care for him so he was disposed of.

The Doctor Arthur case and similar cases raise all kinds of questions about parental responsibility. Parents seem to feel that difficulties created by their children must be removed or remedied by the state. The state has been made responsible and no longer the parents.

With the availability of amniocentises and other tests aimed at preventing the birth of handicapped children, has come the expectation that we have the right to have normal, healthy, perfect children. Perhaps we are no longer prepared to accept imperfection. Genetic engineering is almost a reality. Does imperfection threaten the system scientists are trying to create?

Our culture in the 1980s is one of instant everything: instant meals and entertainment, instant luxury and perfection. Advertising dreams up the perfect home for us with a perfect kitchen and children dressed in whiter-than-white clothes. Perhaps we no longer have the guts to face problems. We have no resources to cope. Gone are the days when people had to face death and suffering frequently. Of course, this is an advance for which we are grateful. But does the current apathy towards the Christian faith remove our very equipment for survival in an imperfect world? We have become too frightened to dare to grow through difficulties. We can't face them at all; we feel that they will overcome us utterly. By trying to remove all possible suffering we may be removing the means by which these events are survived and triumphed over. We cannot control everything; the world will never be a 'safe place'. By encouraging people to expect this, we weaken their ability to survive.

I wondered if the attitude of the parents of handicapped children also affected the level of development the child reached, and the ability of the parents to cope with the child. It appears that the striking contrast between the achievements of Francoise Brinkworth and the girl in the previous film was not related to inate ability but to nurturing and encouragement.

I asked Pat, in the Down's group, about any parents she had known who had rejected their children. She knew of only one couple who had refused to take their baby home from hospital. It was later adopted. Another family had found they had to place their child in a residential placement after the first five years. They said this was due to tensions within the family.

People have spoken about the strain on a marriage and on the other offspring that a handicapped child has brought. Perhaps it is simply that any crisis will show up the weaknesses in a marriage and the difficulties in communicating that a couple have. Mark and I found Elizabeth has drawn us closer to each other; we are by no means unique in this experience.

Other children in a family do need to be helped to accept a handicapped child, but Pat spoke very positively about her teenagers' reactions. She took care to take them out on their own sometimes to do things they particularly enjoyed, but this is probably no different from the way parents would handle normal children of different ages. It seems important not to let the other children feel they must carry 'the burden' of a handicapped child. If the parents don't see that child as a burden perhaps the other children won't either.

If parents' own expectations influence their attitudes to their handicapped children, and the results obtained, then I wonder if expecting other children and parents to reject your child can become a self-fulfilling prophecy. I realize that Elizabeth is young, but in none of the playgroups she attends, nor on a social level, have I ever experienced any kind of rejection by parent or child. If we feel our children are totally acceptable then other people may begin to share those feelings too.

For Mark and me, the sense of God giving us Elizabeth has made a big difference to our sense of responsibility for her. We have no desire to hand her over to other people to be cared for. She is our daughter.

But too, we are fortunate to have the resources to cope with the sadness one is bound to feel. In the Bible we are never told that life will be a bed of roses for the Christian. James and Peter both spoke about the trials that will come to everyone. What we can be sure of is that we will be given the strength to go through these difficulties and not just to survive them, but to learn through them and even triumph in them. We have the reminder before us of the cross and resurrection.

We have found that as we expect good things from Elizabeth, and positive responses from other people, we have got them. Life in an imperfect world can be very exciting and surprising. Perhaps we all need to be more daring in the way we live.

12

First Steps

21st October. Elizabeth at eighteen months

I took Elizabeth to a clergy-wives meeting a couple of weeks ago. I came away feeling discouraged. Elizabeth had been sick half a dozen times on what was clearly a very beautiful carpet. Elizabeth has been sick after breakfast almost every day of her life. I supposed it was caused by her floppy muscles due to Down's syndrome or even to an allergy to milk. For the first time as far as I can remember I found I couldn't cope with the embarrassment and after mopping up the last bit ended up muttering loudly, 'Why can't you be like a normal child.' I felt ashamed afterwards. Elizabeth couldn't help it, and I've discovered since that many normal children have the same problem. It is caused by a faulty sphincter into the stomach, and the sickness often stops when the child walks.

Perhaps this illustrates one of the problems of having a Down's child as one's first baby. A friend who had her Down's child second in the family has often said how she envies me because I have no other child to compare Elizabeth with and so do not get so frustrated if she seems behind. This may be true, but I have also no model of 'normal' behaviour to follow. When Elizabeth was very small I assumed that all her behaviour was due to Down's syndrome.

I have been continually surprised to discover subsequently that her behaviour is very normal and has followed a normal pattern even though more slowly. Other normal children eat paper or pull hair. In fact, it is unusual for Down's children to exhibit peculiar behaviour. They are not mentally disturbed unless something occurs to disturb them. They are well balanced individuals. As Elizabeth has grown older this has become more apparent. She does behave in a socially acceptable fashion, but it has taken me a long time to be confident of this.

Although I have read books in which mothers have blamed their handicapped child for the problems they've encountered, I have never felt it was in any way Elizabeth's fault when life has been difficult. And when Elizabeth herself has been hard to handle it has usually been because she has thrown her dinner on the floor, or crawled away while being dressed. She has tipped her drink on the carpet and enjoyed the pattern it has made. She has blown raspberries and covered my clean dress with yoghurt. I now realize that every child does these things. In fact they have given me a bond with other mothers. It has been a relief to hear someone else describe their toddler's similar behaviour and to know Elizabeth is like everyone else.

My reactions after Elizabeth's birth, my over-sensitivity and depression, I thought at the time were due to the shock of having a handicapped child. Later I realized that, in this too, everyone else shares the same kind of feelings after the major upheaval of giving birth. It surprised me to think that I might not have felt terribly different at times if Elizabeth had been normal. One assumes normality would solve one's problems, but life isn't always that simple.

This month I have noticed that the hair-pulling is less frequent and Elizabeth is gentler and more obedient. She still isn't walking alone, but I bought her some shoes which seem to help her to keep her balance when she walks around the furniture. Today she took a couple of steps on her own. Perhaps this is the start.

26th October

I took Elizabeth to the Pram Club today. The hall is large and noisy and the children roar about on bicycles or push trucks around a ring of chatting mothers. When she was younger Elizabeth found the noise rather disturbing, but she is such a sociable person that she now enjoys seeing the other children. But she still feels happiest viewing them from my lap. When she is walking I expect she will feel more confident.

I put her down on the floor when Mark came in to talk to the mothers; the group meets in the church hall. When Elizabeth saw Mark she walked four whole steps towards him on her own. I was thrilled. I must have shouted out as several women turned to look and probably wondered why I made so much fuss.

I'm not sure why walking is so important, but to see a small child transformed from a crawler to a biped is a major breakthrough. They seem to join the rest of the world and become fully human. Babyhood is left behind. Most of my friends' children began to walk during the period when Elizabeth seemed not to be developing and I felt discouraged when almost everyone I met, at that time, asked if she was walking too. But each day now I feel confident that it won't be too long before she is toddling around like the other children.

The Pram Club has recently started a painting and crayoning corner and I took Elizabeth over to try some artistic experiments. She still eats the paper, but showing her how to hold the crayon and to make marks with it should give her some idea. Being able to use crayons and paint is another milestone. As Elizabeth begins to move towards these milestones I feel that we can do the things together that I dreamed about before she was born. I feel more hopeful. And, yes, more like other mothers; no longer so isolated by the sense that we haven't quite 'made it' into the world of parenthood.

22nd November. Elizabeth at nineteen months

Yesterday Elizabeth walked twenty-two steps on her own. She kept on and on round the sitting-room with a grin of delight on her face. I felt so excited. We all clapped, including Elizabeth. She often claps now to praise herself. I spent one week trying to teach her to point to herself when I asked 'Where is Lizzie?' She touched her tummy in reply, to start with, so I clapped delightedly. The next time I asked her 'Where is Lizzie?' she clapped instead of pointing. I laughed, but I suppose she doesn't understand the question yet.

It seems as if Elizabeth will soon be walking around everywhere, and I feel happy now about her beginning to attend the small playgroup that Chris runs. She asked me to take her along today. I felt as if I had somehow betrayed Elizabeth as I walked away from the clinic door after depositing her with Chris. She was crying and although I knew I'd be returning in an hour, I still felt ashamed as I walked away. These feelings must be with many mothers as they take their children to school or playgroup for the first time. Yet it is irrational. I have left Elizabeth for an hour, before, in the crèche during church services and occasionally with Chris or another friend. Perhaps it isn't just the time involved, but the feeling that leaving Elizabeth at playgroup is the beginning of having to let go of her to others. Her education will no longer be my sole responsibility.

It is a special kind of playgroup, designed for a maximum of ten children, all with some kind of special need. They may be late in talking, or not have much stimulation at home, or may be shy and unused to mixing with other children. Two nursery nurses run the group which is known as 'An Opportunity Group' or 'Play Therapy'. At the moment none of the other children there are handicapped and all are older than Elizabeth, between two and four years old.

I can see again how God has provided us with exactly what we need for Elizabeth at this time. Chris, our Portage visitor, is one of the nursery nurses. Without her enthusiasm and interest in Elizabeth I'm sure she would not have been able to start there until she was over two. By then we would have moved to a new parish. I don't think Elizabeth would be able to cope so well with a strange group run by staff she didn't know. But Elizabeth has known Chris all her life and seen her at least once a week.

When I came to collect Elizabeth after the hour was up, I saw her before she caught sight of me. She was standing at a small table looking at some farm animals that another child was playing with. She looked very grown up. Apparently she had played happily with the other children for the whole session. I was relieved, but also pleased when, as soon as she saw me, she beamed broadly and held out her arms to be cuddled. I felt confident that with Chris's help this would be a very beneficial experience for Elizabeth. I felt very grateful to God for the way it had been arranged.

I pushed Elizabeth home in the buggy, feeling like many of my friends whom I had often seen taking or collecting their children from playgroup. I felt delighted that Elizabeth had at least begun her education with normal children, even if they did have their own special needs. The amount of individual attention available coupled with the stimulation of the language and play of the other children seemed an ideal combination. It could be a useful bridge to the more demanding situation of a larger normal nursery school.

In some ways it is easy for parents of handicapped children to feel like second-class citizens with regard to education. It was not until the 1971 Education Act was passed that handicapped children in England and Wales were required to be formally educated by the state. Before then, the training centres provided concentrated mainly on social skills.

After the passing of this Act, attempts were made to introduce more academic subjects such as reading and writing skills. The policy, however, was for nearly all Down's children to be sent to schools for severely handicapped children (previously known as training centres), regardless of their ability.

Our local Down's group had fought hard for some of the more able children to attend the local ESN (mild) school, and the children were making excellent progress there. But I knew no examples of able Down's children who had spent any time in a normal infant school in our area.

I began to read about schools and came across a fascinating report in a Down's Children's Association monograph called *Let's be positive* by J. R. Ludlow. It was a survey of Down's children contacted through developmental clinics in Kent. Several case studies described parents' successful attempts to teach their children to read at between two and three years old. They also described the effects of normal nursery education. Later some of these children went on to ESN (mild) schools. One attended a PNEU nursery school and then a normal private school where the staff took a particular interest in their first Down's pupil. At age twelve and a half she was finally transferred to an ESN (mild) school. She reads and writes well and has wide interests. I was excited to find a child who had been educated for so long with normal children. She was only one out of many children in the survey, but the results seemed very encouraging. She could only have benefitted from this kind of experience.

But many parents do not have the means for private education. It seems wrong that we have to fight a monolithic system to get a just hearing for our child. Normal children have a right to normal education unless they show evidence of needing some kind of special help. But it seems that for Down's children, we have to prove that they are exceptional in order for the barrier of their label to be disregarded.

Elizabeth might not be able to cope with the pressures of a normal environment but if she shows herself able to do so, it is frightening to feel that preconceived ideas of Down's children's attainments could exclude her from having the opportunity.

But the fight may not be as fierce as we would have found it some years ago. In 1981 another Education Act was passed which aims at encouraging as much integration of handicapped children into normal schools as possible over the next few years. More special units attached to normal schools are planned, where children can go for some lessons while sharing other activities with the rest of the children. An alternative proposal is for there to be extra assistants in normal classes to help the handicapped pupils.

I wondered what teachers' reactions to these proposals might be and was much encouraged when we shared a table at the church harvest supper with a headmaster and his wife, who is also a teacher. Both were much in favour of integration. But still I wonder how common this attitude is.

In an edition of *Parent's Voice*, the magazine of MENCAP, I read a disturbing article about a Down's child who had attended normal nursery school for some time with her mother. When she was formally offered a full-time place at the school, the local authority refused to fund it. The parents were not allowed to pay themselves and the child was sent to an ESN (severe) school on a part-time basis. The nursery had brought obvious advantages to Greer and her mother, not least that of helping them to feel normal members of the community. 'Our fight was over' wrote her mother sadly.

Ulla Bondo has written about her Down's daughter in *Ida*. She attended a normal nursery school, remaining with children younger than herself to begin with and then moving up to be with her own age-group. Later, she found that the remedial class of the normal infant school did not help her, but that she achieved most in a small school in the class two years below that of her age-group. She was provided with an extra teacher to help her with maths and other work. Her language development was good. Unfortunately this experience did not occur in Great Britain.

It seems to be particularly in the area of language development that Down's children would benefit from a normal environment. If they do not tend to 'explode into speech' until four and a half to five years old, rather than at the usual time of around three years, then it is just when they need conversation with their peers that they are removed to an environment where all the other children are also slow to speak. Those children described in the Kent survey who had some experience of normal education also had good language development.

Elizabeth has so far spent a good deal of time with normal

children and she behaves very little differently from other children slightly younger than herself. It seems a pity that she should be removed from an entirely normal environment so soon. Most special schools take children from three years onwards. Later, she may feel happier with friends with the same interests and abilities as herself, but these need not all be handicapped.

I may be blind to my own non-acceptance of Elizabeth's problems and react against the image of ESN (severe) schools with groups of severely handicapped pupils. But Down's children are great imitators and could easily learn subnormal behaviour. Even though they may well need the expert teaching a special school can provide, it seems good to give our children models of normal behaviour to copy.

Not all handicaps need be treated in the same way. Each differs so much in the skills that need to be taught and in those that can be learnt. To place all handicapped children together in the same environment may not always mean that their individual needs are met appropriately.

Comprehensive education means equal opportunities. It seems a betrayal of this ideal to shut all handicapped children away from society, often bussing them some miles to schools in areas unknown to their parents. Small units with specially-trained staff attached to normal schools, like the remedial departments already operating, seem to have advantages. The handicapped children can join in activities appropriate to them and the barriers of fear and ignorance could be greatly reduced if normal children get to know handicapped children as friends. Their parents, too, could feel a part of the community rather than being ostracized in some way.

I have heard of examples of handicapped children in normal infant schools being provided with an extra assistant to help with reading and maths. I hope for that kind of situation for Elizabeth.

Perhaps the fact that I am a teacher too, makes it harder for me to let go of my own child's education. But when much of my energy is, at present, directed to finding new ways to stimulate Elizabeth and much of my time is spent in trying to provide her with new and helpful experiences, it seems harder to let go and impossible to give her up to a system of education that I fear will not develop her potential to the full.

Shortly after Elizabeth was born, I had stronger feelings about educating Elizabeth myself. It may have been part of my fear that people would try to take her away from me. I feel now that it is essential that she learns from other children and from other teachers. But I need, too, to feel we are all working for Elizabeth's best interests.

Perhaps these thoughts and fears are some way from the playgroup she began this morning, but they are the thoughts and emotions that come whenever 'education' as an issue looms before us.

Perhaps I am too optimistic. Many other parents in the local group fear the rejection their child might suffer from normal children and would rather keep them in a more sheltered environment. I still think of the book I read recently by Hannah Musset called *The Untrodden Ways* in which she admitted to wanting to kill her Down's baby because she believed that society would reject her and society was not ready to change. If people are given the opportunity to really know handicapped children of all kinds, is it too optimistic to believe that they might respond with love and understanding rather than with fear?

For Elizabeth to live confidently in a difficult world perhaps she needs the challenges of a normal environment for as long as she can happily cope with it. Perhaps too, the 'normal environment' needs to dare to accept the challenge of living with handicapped people.

13

Other Handicaps

When Elizabeth was about nine months old, I gave in to the repeated reminders from members of the Down's group to take Elizabeth swimming. The Down's group had persuaded a local school for severely handicapped children to open its excellent pool to mothers of pre-school handicapped children, once a week.

Elizabeth gradually gained confidence in the water, learning to keep her head up and to move her legs about. Over the space of a few months, as she relaxed, I was able to let her float and splash about on her own, supported by a ring and arm-bands. We became quite a spectacle in the pool as she splashed about shouting 'da, da, da'! I expect the echo encouraged her; the other children seemed quite quiet in comparison. It was good exercise for Elizabeth and she usually fell asleep as we drove home.

As we went to the pool week by week, I too learnt new things. I met mothers of children with a variety of handicaps and began to understand a little of what life must be like for them. There was a four-year-old boy with spina bifida, unable to walk, but quite a competent swimmer. I made what was, I suppose, a common mistake when I first saw him. I didn't realize that despite his wheelchair he is of normal intelligence and can speak well. I asked his mother, over his head, how old he was. I felt ashamed when he answered, realizing how frustrating it must be for him to be treated as if he is mentally handicapped just because he can't walk.

A tiny girl with only one eye used to come swimming. She was of a similar age to Elizabeth, but couldn't sit up or move around. She had a brain growth. Her mother would hold her in the warm water for the entire session, where the child usually fell asleep. I felt sad for her. The child died shortly after her mother gave birth to twins. I was glad it hadn't happened before this. The mother was devastated. Now, at least, she had a new focus to her life.

Two brothers were often at the pool. Their handicap was rare and little was known about it. The older one did not speak and both had various behavioural problems. Their mother was always cheerful and friendly yet they were very difficult to manage. It must also have been hard to come to terms with the fact that theirs was a genetic disorder and she was unlikely to have normal children.

There were several children with cerebral palsy; various degrees of brain damage. One mother explained sadly that her pretty three-year-old had been severely damaged at birth. She was developmentally a long way behind normal now. To know that one's child could have been so different, but for a mistake or accident, must be hard to face. Anger and bitterness could easily be all one felt.

I felt grateful that Elizabeth had Down's syndrome. I knew nothing could ever have been done to prevent it. We had no regrets about a damaging delivery, an accident on an operating table, no 'If only that hadn't happened'. I imagine that depression must be a common consequence of the unresolved conflicts and anger that many parents feel in these situations. It was much simpler for us. We knew to some extent what we could expect in the future for Elizabeth. With other handicaps the future is often totally unpredictable.

Several mothers were pregnant and most were determined to have amniocentises. Coming to a school where the pupils were severely handicapped made one feel that there were many handicapped children in the world. But because this was a centre for quite a large area the picture must have been a little distorted.

I felt sure that if I became pregnant I did not want the test done. I couldn't have an abortion. I didn't feel I could stand in judgement on another's life and say, 'No, life will not be worth living for you. You cannot have this experience.' Meeting the boy with spina bifida made me feel wary of decisions to abort babies with such a disease. I understood that the level of spina bifida varies, but he clearly had a large potential for fulfilment in life. Being unable to walk hardly seems a reason for not living.

When I saw severely brain-damaged babies and older children in wheelchairs, I found it harder to think about. But often these handicaps are not genetically caused. The children often are normal until birth. We cannot know what life will be like for them either. But I can understand now why placing such a child in residential care might be the best decision for parent and child. If the child's development never progresses beyond that of a baby, it must be impossible for the mother to live a normal life with the child. A baby who never grows older makes huge demands on a mother.

A book that helped me to appreciate the problems

involved more sympathetically, was about a boy called Zachariah. I realized then that all handicaps need to be considered individually. Zachariah was a severely brain-damaged child who was unable to sit up, speak or move very much. Eventually he also became blind.

Fern Kupfer, Zach's mother, described many initial feelings after his birth that I also identified with. She felt that his birth redefined her life. In the first year after his birth she would walk around the house picking up a photograph or a glass and say, 'This was taken before Zach was born . . . Oh I bought that after Zach was born.' She saw two lives separated by an event that had irreversible consequences.

> Zach has changed me and sometimes I can no longer
> think of who I was before I had this identity. . .
> Radicalized, I have fought for Zach's rights and for our
> rights as a family to survive. I know I am stronger for
> the struggle and perhaps I am a better person. A woman
> who has a Down's syndrome child told me that 'having
> a handicapped child is the best self-assertiveness training
> course there is.' But oh, I did not sign up for this
> course. This was an elective not of my own choosing.

Fern went on to describe the problem of accepting one's child.

> A few years ago I hurt whenever I saw a baby crawling
> and cooing and doing cute baby things. A few weeks ago
> I saw a blond curly-headed little boy in overalls and tiny
> red sneakers running across the campus towards his
> Mom. The image, recalled over and over again that day,
> tore at me . . . I don't know if you ever totally learn
> to accept it. I know that Zach is irreparably damaged.
> I accept that. And yet, at the very core, I still find the
> whole situation somewhat unbelievable, and yes,
> unacceptable. Once a parent at a support meeting for
> handicapped children with a retarded teenager said,
> 'Well, it took me a long time but I *have* learned to
> accept it – about twenty-eight days out of the month.'

Fern spoke of her delight at eventually being offered some constructive help for Zach. A neuro-developmental therapy programme was to be held during one summer vacation. Fern and Joe decided to take Zach. They planned to each take three-week stretches, alternating between looking after Zach, and then working at home and caring for their daughter Gabi.

Sadly, the progress made on the programme was not to last. It was eventually discovered that Zach had a degenerative disease and would die in a few years time. As he deteriorated it became impossible for the family to cope with him all the time. In order to do so, they had to work a kind of shift pattern so that someone was always with Zach. He began to spend spells of time in residential care. Fern described the pain of his returns at weekends.

> The 'visits' made me a little crazy – like an intense affair
> you know should end, no future in it. Why prolong
> the pleasure and the pain. . . ? Still, my overwhelming
> feeling when I took him back . . . the biggie feeling
> that washed over the regulars of anger and grief and
> guilt . . . was relief. And the realization of this is proof
> to me that for my own life I'll be 'doing the right thing'
> by trying to get Zach into a residential place as soon
> as possible.

A permanent home was found, where Zach was well cared for. When it was confirmed that Zach probably didn't have many years to live, Fern wrote:

> Intellectually, I know it will be better for Zach's life to
> end, it's too cruel for him to grow physically, only to
> become a giant infant who can do nothing at all.
> Emotionally, however, I feel a real sense of loss, so
> sorry about the whole travesty that was his life,
> apologetic to him for having to put him through it.

Fern was not a Christian, but she admired the strength a Christian friend of hers showed with her similarly handicapped son. Fern said, 'Would that I could believe in angels, then in another time and place he could be whole and at peace.' She had a dream one night. She saw Zach sitting in his chair as she came in from outside. Zach spoke,

> 'Hi,' he said gently. It was Zach's voice, and though he
> has said not a word in his life, I know it was the voice
> he would have if he could talk. 'Can you say, "Hi
> Mommy"? ' I asked surprised. . . 'Hi Mommy' he said
> and then raised an eyebrow as if to add, 'How's that?'

Near the end of the book, Fern wrote:

> There were no days when Zach lived with us for those
> two years and four months that I felt on top of the
> world. And I must say . . . that I think if he had lived
> with us for the next two years, the world would have
> crushed me. Zach and the fact of who Zach is will always
> make me unutterably sad, and it is something that I
> have come to live with, those fantasy flashes of who he
> could have been. But these are brief; they rest now in
> a smaller space of who I am.

I cried as I read. It was not difficult to imagine the tremendous pain Fern must have suffered and to know that she had few resources outside of herself to make sense of it all. Yet she experienced the same joy that we did when Zach learnt something new in those early days, and she too wondered at the responses he was able to make to her. She knew how much she loved him.

The power to love seems to be a gift which is able to overcome all outward appearances. How can people care, day by day, for children so damaged that they will never grow up? Sometimes I wonder if the gift of love is not one of the most powerful evidences for the existence of God in the world. Where does it come from, this force that feels no bounds as it looks down at that tiny damaged person and sees a human soul?

Love was perhaps what motivated the work Ann's parents carried out to enable her to become almost a normal young woman by the time she was twenty-one despite the fact that she was autistic. They persevered when no help was available from specialists for autistic children. The book *For the love of Ann* by James Copeland with Jack Hodges, ends when Ann is about to find her first job as a secretary. The changes wrought in her life during the years since she was a withdrawn, disturbed child, are amazing.

To love is to be happy with by Barry Kaufman tells of an American family's battle to communicate with an autistic boy against professional advice. A rigorous eight-hour daily programme of stimulation and teaching was begun by his parents and after about a year brought Raun, the small boy, to a developmental level comparable with that of his young peers. The greatest breakthrough was in the area of speech. His parents had sought to enter his world, and to draw him into ours, through their love and acceptance, and it worked.

These people did not claim to have any particular faith in God, yet I felt I had much in common with their desire to love and accept their child despite the pressures from society to do otherwise. Perhaps my sense of God's control of our lives, and the way he continues to bring good out of every aspect of Elizabeth's existence, helps me especially when I am tempted to give up my resolve. I couldn't love and care for Elizabeth and rejoice in her without God's power to enable me to. I am indeed fortunate.

As I think about the handicaps other children and their parents have to bear, I continue to be grateful that Elizabeth has Down's syndrome. Many of my emotions are similar to those of parents with differently handicapped children, but there is a simplicity for us too. We know that Elizabeth will be able to learn quite a lot and will walk and talk. She, in her own way, will be a complete person, even if different from us. Other handicaps do not promise such a future.

Elizabeth has opened a door for me into another world: a world of damaged children and of parents who have coped courageously with their problems. I feel much sympathy and, yet too, long that those who do not yet know the love and power of God will find this added source of strength and a means of making some sense of the tragedy that has befallen them. That they too can find the joy that lives in sorrow.

14

Struggle for Acceptance

December. Elizabeth at twenty months
I was dreading my first visit to the antenatal clinic since having Elizabeth. I think I put off having this pregnancy confirmed because I feared the trauma of it all. I was sure I would be pressurized into having an amniocentisis and I

didn't want one. I didn't want a question mark to hang over the pregnancy. If the test showed a possible problem and I knew I would never have an abortion then I would rather not have the test at all. There seemed, too, to be some risk of a miscarriage occurring as a result of the test itself.

Eventually the day arrived and I left Elizabeth at a friend's to play with her small boy, then set off. Every time I enter the hospital drive a kind of sick feeling wafts over me. It is impossible not to remember the emotions that were part of my first stay there.

In fact the staff could not have been more helpful and I felt grateful to God for his help over this particular hurdle. The sister suggested I should not even have the blood test if I didn't want the amniocentesis. The consultant who saw me reluctantly agreed for me not to have the test and did not place undue pressure on me. It helped, too, that the houseman on duty had been the same one to tell me I was fit to leave hospital with Elizabeth eighteen months before. He had been very kind to me then. Seeing him first helped me to feel more confident when I spoke to the consultant.

The woman taking my blood for the routine haemaglobin level checks was not so helpful. She spoke about the dreadful suffering of children with spina bifida (the disease the blood test and amniocentisis were used to detect). She thought abortions were the best answer, despite my comment on the varying effects of spina bifida, sometimes being in a very mild form. When she discovered about Elizabeth's handicap she told me how over-affectionate Down's children were. An image of large handicapped adults giving inappropriate and embarrassing cuddles zoomed before me like a spectre. Elizabeth didn't seem to be like this now. She was friendly, but also very keen to establish her independence. My confidence in my decision to refuse the tests was becoming a little shaky as I drove home.

A phone call to a close friend helped me. She too had made a similar decision after her first pregnancy. A blood test then had suggested the need to test for spina bifida. The amniocentisis showed no abnormalities but the anxiety involved in the weeks of waiting for test results was great. Added to this was the agony of knowing a decision might have to be made about an abortion and the fear of a miscarriage occuring as a possible outcome of the test itself. This made my friend decide to refuse the tests a second time. She had experienced the fear of embarking on a second pregnancy with limited reassurance that it was proceeding normally, but said that her confidence grew as the baby began to move and get bigger.

30th December

Just after Christmas the friends we had visited on Elizabeth's first birthday came for lunch. I enjoyed seeing my goddaughter again. She had changed a great deal. She was now the responsible older sister of a three-month-old baby and obviously understood much of what was talked about.

Seeing the two Elizabeths together helped me to have a new understanding of how Down's syndrome affects children. My Elizabeth seemed to have a simplicity that normal children lacked. She could not understand the complicated instructions given to the other child, nor did she show the same initiative. Her speech was a long way behind.

I was interested in my Elizabeth's gentleness with the new baby and her great interest in people. She was very sympathetic after pinching my face and finding out that it hurt me. Her cheekiness, and delight in changing television programmes were other aspects of her simplicity. I enjoyed seeing the two children together and understanding their differences. I suppose it also helped to keep my feet on the ground about our daughter's progress.

31st December

Earlier in December I took Elizabeth to the Health Clinic for her eighteen-month check. For days beforehand I had helped Elizabeth to build three bricks into a tower, knowing that this was one of the tests usually carried out. When we arrived she was examined physically. A few questions were asked about what she could do and that was all. I was puzzled.

Perhaps the doctor didn't test much at this age. Perhaps she had assumed Elizabeth couldn't do anything. At least she saw her walk into the room holding my hand.

A week later I asked the health visitor about it and she looked at Elizabeth's card. The wrong section had been filled in. She hadn't had a proper check at all. I felt annoyed. Why did my child have to be treated differently? I asked if she could be examined again.

I didn't know for what purpose the cards were kept or used. A fear lurked at the back of my mind about reports that might bar her way in to normal education. I expect I was worrying too much, but a further appointment was made.

When we arrived today I felt relieved. Toys were set out at a table and white balls of various sizes were lying on a black cloth on the floor. A nurse was present as well. Perhaps this would be different.

Elizabeth's sight and hearing were tested and pronounced good. I was delighted, as often catarrh in Down's children can cause hearing problems. But I felt disappointed about the rest of the tests.

Elizabeth is good at picture recognition and enjoys books, but this was not revealed because of the kind of questions asked. Her lack of ability to speak and to name several familiar objects was the real observation made. No credit was given for her understanding and appropriate use of the objects. My mind went blank and I felt helpless. I didn't know how to explain what her abilities were.

Is it just that I find it hard to accept her slowness when compared with others, or is it also the lack of understanding of the handicap that the doctor showed? Her assessment by the educational psychologist when she is two will be the really valuable one.

Nagging at me with my feeling of being humiliated in front of the doctor was the accusation that my pride was hurt. But I know I have no right to a bright child and I did nothing to earn any abilities I was given. I know Elizabeth will never be normal, and I can't strive to make her something she cannot be.

But I felt that Elizabeth herself was not appreciated for who she is. Her gifts, such as they are, were not noticed. That was the disappointment. I want people to share the delight we have in Elizabeth and not to write her off because she can't do certain activities at a certain moment in time.

January. Elizabeth at twenty-one months

I felt as if a minor breakthrough occurred this month. One morning after breakfast Elizabeth behaved in a way I would describe as being particularly characteristic of a handicapped child. She sat on the floor by the door into the kitchen and banged her head against it several times. Then she rocked backwards and forwards for a few minutes. It didn't last long and I suppose one could say she was just experimenting with parts of her body. It is not obsessive behaviour and it occurs very rarely. But I laughed.

I found myself thinking that this is typical behaviour of a handicapped child and I don't care. I really don't. I love Elizabeth. I felt that in that moment a greater acceptance of her handicap had crystallized in my mind. I felt happy; there is a freedom in knowing that I don't mind. I love Elizabeth exactly as she is.

Since Christmas and the week away in Cornwall that followed, Elizabeth has made good progress with the Portage activities. It is exciting to see her walking confidently and climbing the stairs. She points to objects around the room when we name them and to pictures in books. Her imaginative play is developing too. Dolls have drinks, cuddles and even a good-night kiss when they are tucked up in bed.

The Christmas parties were opportunities to see how her social skills were developing. At the Pram Club party we sat in a large circle while Mark, dressed as Father Christmas, gave out the presents. Elizabeth watched carefully as each child went up and was delighted when it was her turn. I wondered, foolishly, if she recognized Mark beneath the cotton wool beard. She was certainly pleased to collect her present.

We went to the party for mentally-handicapped children after Christmas. Elizabeth joined in the disco dancing enthusiastically and even watched the conjuror for some time. Her pleasure in collecting her present was clear too. This second Christmas, Elizabeth was more aware of the events despite not understanding their significance.

Bedtimes are now becoming times of hilarity. Elizabeth rushes into the wrong room, shouting with glee, while I follow on with her night-clothes. My enlarging stomach slows my progress considerably. There is still no interest in using a potty but laughter always follows accidents on the floor.

This month I was asked to speak about Elizabeth at two young wives groups. I had never done this before and wondered what it would be like. I prepared a summary of what Down's syndrome meant, what Elizabeth's problems were likely to be and what I had learnt through having her. I ended with the quotation from the book *Small Ship, Great Sea* by T. de Vries-Kruyt that I had found so helpful earlier on.

One of the groups, in particular, moved me by their response and caring attitude. I felt understood and accepted by them. I was asked whether I was afraid for Elizabeth as she grew older; afraid of unkind words and bullying from other children. I said that I wasn't at the moment. I believe that as each new situation arises God will guide and support us as he has in the past. There are bound to be problems but I don't wish to live in fear of them.

Fears for the future, however, do seem something that cloud many parents lives. A friend found her first visits to the Down's group difficult and they were often followed by periods of depression. She worried that her child would acquire all the problems that other children had, rolled into one. Would her child wake at night, even though she didn't now? Would she run away all the time or be impossible to control? Would schools and society in general reject her? Could the parents cope?

The only way I have found to cope with these kind of fears is to read about the lives of Down's children. *Small Ship, Great Sea*, with its details of Jan Maarten's life until he was into his late twenties, allayed many fears. It is important, too, to live in the present and to enjoy our children now. God has helped us month by month through discouraging and exciting times. I cannot believe this help will come to an end.

But perhaps we do end up thinking about the future more than other parents do. Other parents may dream about weddings and grand-children. We need some kind of reality to replace these dreams which were shattered at our children's birth. We have to think hard about what will happen when we die, whether prematurely or in old age. We have to think ahead into a world which may not even exist in twenty, thirty, forty years time. If it does, it is hard to imagine the kind of changes that will have occurred in it. But we need to draw up wills that will provide for our children who cannot inherit or own land or property.

We had a helpful, if sombre, meeting of the Down's group in the autumn when a solicitor explained how trusts can be set up and how the provision of guardians could help our children. (More up-to-date details can be found in the book *After I'm Gone* by Gerald Sanctuary, legal advisor to MENCAP.)

At the moment, the opportunities for permanent care of our children are more varied than ever before. There are state-run institutions. There are also settlements and communities growing up which aim at providing sheltered work and accommodation and a community life for each individual according to his ability.

I was interested in a new development called 'The Christian concern for the mentally handicapped' (see appendix) which is opening houses and workshops in different parts of the country. These are all closely linked with local Baptist churches. The Christian emphasis in this scheme impressed me. There are many other settlements and villages, and names and addresses are available from MENCAP.

It seems right that as one's other children leave home to get jobs or to marry, the handicapped child too should leave to make a new home for themselves, as did Kathy in the programme *Kathy leaves home*. This will then be their home for life, not suddenly lost after the death of parents.

These kind of establishments are in great demand and places are few. An alternative situation is for the child to remain at home after full-time education has ended and to work at a sheltered workshop or in the local community itself, or to live in a hostel in the local community.

Questions spring to mind about how a child's social life would develop. Friends of one's own and a life of one's own are so important if one is to gain some kind of independence. Yet balanced against this is the possible trauma of entering into a community of only handicapped people after living life in a normal environment, where integration has been the aim.

These are questions we cannot answer now. We can think about them, but I trust that as God has given us Elizabeth and the wherewithal to care for her until now, he will provide for each stage. He is faithful and unchanging. How good to know this in an ever-changing world.

15

Why Did It Happen?

I went to a pantomine last night; the stage was filled with tiny trim figures in miniature ballet tutus with lace tights and hair in buns. They weren't all beautiful little girls, but their faces were bright and sparkling as they responded to the excitement of the occasion.

I found it hard to watch, wondering, despite my hopes for Elizabeth, if she would ever look so attractive. But it was more than an outward appearance. As the show continued, older pupils performed and I saw before me the span of her life and I felt the difference in opportunity. I do not have illusions that Elizabeth will be less happy than these young people. I believe she is an essentially happy and contented child. But suddenly, as I turned to look at a row of handicapped young adults who had been brought to the show by those caring for them, it all seemed so unfair. The contrast was suddenly writ large.

Deep down inside, as the tears stopped running silently down my cheeks in the darkness, I knew that Elizabeth's life would not be of less meaning or value than these children's. I suppose fairness has little to do with meaning or fulfilment in life. The children on the stage, because of their very potential, would have more to live up to. I thought of Jesus' words, in Luke 12: 'To whom much is given, much will be required.' We will never all be treated identically in life; we would not really wish to be. The variety of gifts and experiences that we have to offer others is part of the richness of human life. It is, too, the result of the unequal suffering that we all endure.

From a human point of view there are several ways we can make sense of the kind of life Elizabeth will live. One day, while visiting the library, I discovered a book called *Children in Need of Special Care* by Thomas J. Weihs. I left the library walking on air, thrilled that someone could have written so positively about something I believed in too. In a chapter entitled 'The Mongol Child', he wrote:

> People behave today as though sexuality and intellect were achievements of this century . . . sex and intellect are taking possession. . . They occupy an unprecedented position in society. Then in all this, the mongol child appears – loving, innocent, unintellectual, helpless and so very appealing. . . Has not the mongol (come) to provide a medicine rather than to be an illness in our time? Does he not signify something we ought to learn to understand, to accept, and to love for the sake of our own development as man?

Later he wrote:

> Scientific advance will make it possible soon to prevent the birth of mongol children by early detection . . . will we gain by this. . . ? Are we perhaps trying to do away with the medicine before we have derived the full benefit from it? When such thoughts assume the proportions of experience, one encounters the mongol child differently. One does not see only the pathology of his condition. In him one meets a new brother.

He continued by describing how mongol children could help in the education of children with other handicaps. Because they are blissfully unaware of the lack of response from autistic children, they manage to overcome the isolation and withdrawal that autistic children manifest. They can help make severely maladjusted children feel wanted because of their enormous capacity for sympathy and forgiveness. He concluded by saying:

103

I do not mean that I want the mongol child to be a mongol, but that we shall learn to live with him and accept him as one of us, different and yet essentially, deeply, utterly human – as, in fact, our brother.

Already I knew something of Elizabeth's sympathy and forgiveness. She had a short memory when I lost my temper with her, and when I lay for a week on the settee with 'flu she kept walking up to me and giving me cuddles. She seemed concerned, in a way which surprised me for her twenty-two months. Perhaps her acceptance of me had in some way helped to heal my own sadness at her birth.

I was glad that my middle name is Elizabeth, as I thought about what Thomas Weihs had written. I can remember the effort involved, in the early days after her birth, to hold her consciously in my mind as a part of myself. The effort seemed to be necessary to overcome the nagging fear that I might reject her. It was important from the start that we shared the same name. As the months passed she has indeed become, in our eyes, an expression of ourselves, her parents, and yet also something more: 'essentially, deeply human'.

Being a Christian has helped to add a further dimension to my understanding of suffering, of why handicaps occur and particularly, why Elizabeth. I think that lives that are damaged in some way are part, theologically speaking, of a fallen world. Man turned away from God, right at the very start of his existence on earth. He wanted his independence, to be in control of his own destiny. Yet in that turning away, he separated himself from the relationship of unity, trust and love with God which would have given him the peace of mind and direction he strove for. The result of this turning away, which is something that mankind has continued to do ever since, is conflict with his fellow man and disorder and conflict in the whole universe; thorns and thistles grow, it seems, symbolically, to remind us of man's struggle to be at home in the world. They remind us that we all suffer, to some degree, because we are often too proud to admit that we cannot live without God.

In some sense, all handicap, distortion, illness and imperfection is part of a world bearing its sentence; a self-imposed isolation from a loving creator. But God has not withdrawn himself, and he is at work for restoration and healing in the very places where man's rebellion and its results are most obviously manifested.

I have never felt that God wanted Elizabeth to be born with the limitations she has; nor does he wish any suffering for any of his creatures. But when God made man he made him with a freedom of choice. He took a risk. He did not create robots, programmed to love him; and man was free to choose to live without him if he so wished. Man's choice has consequences which are obvious in our society and we cannot turn round and blame God for them. We cannot blame God for unequal distribution of wealth, disease due to neglect and social diseases due to injustice and lack of compassion. In the wider world we cannot blame God that two thirds of the world starves while the remainder live with plenty to spare.

Given an imperfect world, God does not give up, but uses suffering as part of his restoring and redeeming plan for the world. In some way, Elizabeth bears in herself the pain man bears as part of his self-chosen separation from God. She has no choice. Yet, as Christ bore the sins of the world in innocence, and through his death brought life to all who will accept it, so Elizabeth's life can be used by God as part of his redemptive plan. He can use her to change us, her parents, to heal the distortions and false ambitions that we hold dear. He can use her to change our narrow view of our lives and of others and to form in us a more Christ-like character.

Being like Jesus is the only way to be fully human. He is the only truly human being who has ever lived. He was not distorted by the self-centredness and sin that affects us all. He was truly free and chose to obey his Father God utterly. In that obedience he suffered isolation, rejection, physical pain and death. He suffered for the truth and he suffered to enable us to know God for ourselves. So suffering is part of being human. In Hebrews chapter 5 it says that 'Jesus learnt obedience by the things that he suffered.' If this was true for Jesus, how much more is it necessary for us. From a personal point of view we could say Elizabeth was given us to teach us obedience. To teach us obedience to God's way of seeing things – to help us remove the idols of intelligence, success, self acclaim that pull us away from worshipping and loving God alone.

Because of the way we are encouraged to look at the world today we tend not to see suffering as a valuable part of life. We are encouraged to see illness as a curse to be immediately remedied by antibiotics, and death as the greatest enemy. We try to make it more palatable by distancing ourselves from it. We make it unreal by screening violence and murder on television. We watch film massacres and suffering occuring hundreds or thousands of miles away, too far from home to affect us. We legalize the abortion of imperfect children or children who may cause us pain in other ways. Perhaps we have misunderstood. We cannot protect ourselves, as if by right, from hurt and pain. Maybe the only way is to enter into suffering as we enter into life and to accept suffering as a valuable part of life: a place where we can discover the reality that is God, and the depths of his love.

I was struck by some lines in a book called *Song for Sarah* by Paula D'Arcy. The book is a collection of letters written by a mother to her child before and after her birth and then after her tragic death.

Ironically, neither pain nor happiness were true indicators that he (God) was or was not there, though often I mistakenly thought that too. His purposes work together in *all* conditions of life, if we could only see. . . I ached and sorrowed so at losing you. But the pain, in the end, did not have the final say. . .

There are many things people say when a disaster strikes them. 'If there is a God, he wouldn't allow this.' 'If God is a God of love he wouldn't allow this.' 'Why did God punish me by making this happen?' I think we sometimes get stuck at these questions and never move on into a deeper understanding of reality. In that moving on is healing.

If we look at the cross we begin to see suffering not as something God gives us to bear, but something he shares with us. This year we had a communion service on the Sunday morning before Christmas day. I found it a particularly moving occasion. I thought about Jesus as God's Son, existing with God in eternity before his birth on earth. I began to realize that he did not allow himself to be born a man out of nowhere, in a vacuum. He came because he loved us. Heaven is not a place removed from suffering and grief. God is aware intimately of all the pain and grief and human agony ever suffered by any man. God sent his Son and Jesus came willingly, because this was the only solution to the pain of the world. God has shared that pain ever since creation and Jesus' coming was part of that sharing. A verse in John's Gospel, chapter 3, sums it up. 'God loved the world so much that he gave his only Son so that everyone who believes in him may not die but have eternal life.'

We can never turn to God and say, 'You do not understand – you cannot know the pain and loss.' I believe God feels our pain more fully than we do ourselves. We have an inkling of this when our own children suffer. We would willingly exchange places with them. We suffer the pain of not being able to stop the suffering and yet wanting to help so much.

When Jesus became man and shared our life, he suffered the pain of isolation and misunderstanding and physical pain. But worse, he eventually suffered the rejection of his Father in order that our sins could be dealt with. I wonder if we will ever understand a small part of what that meant. Our relationships are so imperfect and marred with our own selfishness that we find it hard to conceive of a perfect unity shared by two people. It is harder still to know what it must have felt like for that unity to be shattered, even momentarily.

Jesus' death means life and forgiveness and freedom for us who could never deserve or earn it for ourselves. God's love has gone to such limits that we can no longer say to him, 'It isn't fair' when something awful happens to us. Fairness seems a poor way to argue with someone so generous in their self-giving.

But I suppose that even these thoughts have taken two years to crystallize and are only small pieces of a far greater jigsaw puzzle. It is a great help to begin to see suffering as a part of a bigger plan with a larger purpose than we can grasp. But one has to hold on tenaciously to the sanity and meaning within a seemingly pointless tragedy. When the event happens it may overwhelm us with its grief. Only later can we stagger out into the weak sunlight and think a little more clearly about it. We may even begin to see that very suffering as a special kind of blessing.

Sometimes now it is easy to forget the early pain of having Elizabeth. Intellectually I know that our suffering over her is small compared with that of many others in the world. Yet I know that what we have learnt through her seems to be great riches, and who we have, this small person, seems of infinite value. We cannot say 'Is it fair?' but instead, 'Thank you for letting us learn all this.'

Suffering may well be a neutral event in itself. It is from its effects on us that good or bad can result. We can become bitter, angry, resentful, twisted and hurt inside, never allowing ourselves to find healing. Or we can accept what happens to us trustingly, believing that God can use even this for good in some way.

I wouldn't be honest if I said that 'accepting suffering trustingly' was really possible without God's help. Nor as human beings that we consistently maintain this attitude. But when Elizabeth was born God seemed to take over and show me a way through. He was there. I didn't make myself accept anything. I couldn't. Yet as I read the Bible and as I thought about my life up until that moment, I felt I could see a meaning. God gave me a window to look through. He can do this for anyone.

The last two years have been a kind of see-saw. Sometimes it is easy to be grateful for our situation and I can see something of what we learn from it. Elizabeth herself is a source of encouragement and fun. But sometimes I need to discipline myself to hold on to what I know to be the truth. It seems to be almost a habit of mind.

There have been times when my feelings have spiralled downwards. One small thing after another sucks me downwards towards doubt and depression. 'I've got a handicapped child – isn't that enough.' But I know that is only an excuse for self-indulgence, and is different from letting real pain come out and be expressed. To do that is a healing thing; to cry and yet find relief in the tears. The downward spirals, on the other hand, need to be recognized for what they are.

This sense of discipline, the habit of mind we develop, was strangely echoed in something Mark wrote in his diary on the day before Elizabeth was born. It still never ceases to amaze me how much God was in control of this event and how he prepared us both for her. This is what Mark wrote:

9th April
'Endure hardship as discipline' (Hebrews 12:7).
Doubtless this job involves very little real hardship but nonetheless it isn't always an easy life, so it's good to know that there is discipline at work here, and that in turn discipline 'produces a harvest of righteousness and peace for those who have been trained by it'. But discipline must not be 'made light of'. I suppose one way of making light of God's discipline is not to recognize it as such, to see hardship as merely a tedious fact of life without real significance. I suppose one might say that the real secret lies in one's attitudes. One can treat life as full of the inexplicable and so chafe against it, or, one can accept anything that is hard to understand or cope with as a form of God's discipline. That way nothing is not capable of being turned to good account.

Because Mark has seen something of the purpose in Elizabeth's life and has not spent time feeling sorry for himself or us, he has helped me to hold before me the reality of the situation. We have both been very sad sometimes, but Mark has never been bitter or angry and I am always grateful for this.

Other entries in Mark's diary show that God gave to Mark 'a way of seeing' just as he gave it to me. The foundation we share gives a security and strength to me which perhaps I take far too much for granted.

11th April
Funny how I should have read and written what precedes this the day before what happened, whatever it was – and that we don't know for sure yet – yesterday. 'Nothing is not capable of being turned to good

account'. God grant that if this child is a mongol he may turn that to really good account, that his name may be glorified. . .

13th April

Yesterday was Sunday and the epistle was from 1 Corinthians 1. What struck me was verse 25: 'the foolishness of God is wiser than men; and the weakness of God is stronger than men'. Surely this all ties up with the strange (i.e. 'foolish') idea that this little girl is a trust from God. We are tempted to say, 'It's all a mistake', or more theologically, 'It's part of the fallenness of nature.' But we seem to feel that she was meant and we cannot intellectually comprehend that because the foolishness of God is wiser than men. All suffering, and of course supremely the suffering of the cross, is part of the foolishness of God. It doesn't make intellectual, philosophical sense, but at a deeper level it's wisdom is palpable. And so, of course, to suffer is to be close to God, because in some way we are able to see, without being able to explain, what he is doing in the world. . .

Those last words express closely how I feel; 'to suffer is to be close to God because in some way we are able to see, without being able to explain, what he is doing in the world. . .' We can't explain. I can't present a neatly packaged answer as to why suffering occurs. I can only share what we have learnt through Elizabeth, the insight and blessing as well as the pain. The whole experience has made me feel that God is far bigger than we might imagine, and more in control of our lives than we realize when everything seems to go wrong around us. It has opened up to me the pain of others and helped me to identify with many more people than I was able to before. Perhaps I am a more vulnerable person. We are keen to hide our pain and like to appear to be 'copers', strong people. But true sharing with another human being involves being vulnerable and honest. We have to learn this honesty that makes for real relationships rather than just the appearance of such.

We have no choice about the kind of suffering that is given to us. If we did, we would not choose the experience nor the lessons that we needed to learn from it. But afterwards we can sometimes begin to understand why it has happened. When Elizabeth was born, a dream was shattered. But God was there and gently held together the pieces of our lives until they began to mend a little. Mary Craig, in her book *Blessings*, wrote of the continuous experience we all have of being broken up and put together again. It seems to me to be part of the transforming, renewing work of the Holy Spirit. Romans 12 speaks of not being conformed to the world (or pressed into its mould) but being transformed 'by the renewing of your mind. Then you will know what is God's will.' 1 Peter 1 says, 'Now for a little while you may have had to suffer grief in all kinds of trials. These have come so that your faith – of greater worth than gold . . . may be proved genuine and may result in praise, glory and honour when Jesus Christ is revealed.'

When a tragedy happens, it is easy to feel that the world has collapsed for ever at our feet, that all is chaos and life has gone out of control. But when that point was reached for me after Elizabeth's birth, I found that God was there. He was still that rock deep within. He will be there when the world falls again.

We have no insurance policy against being hurt, but we do have a God who has been there before us and is in the pain with us. He is a God who could not remain isolated from his creation. He had to become a man and share life with us. He is the God who walked in the fiery furnace with Daniel and his friends. He is the God of the cross, but also of the resurrection. Psalm 46 says,

'God is our refuge and strength,
    a well proved help in trouble.
Therefore we will not fear though the earth should change.
        Though the mountains shake in the heart of the sea.'

16

Breakthrough

February. Elizabeth at twenty-two months
February is always a grey month for me. And cold, as if winter cannot bear to leave and let spring bring everything to life again. This February has been no exception, with post 'flu depression lurking darkly each morning and increasing tiredness as the pregnancy progresses.

These feelings were intensified in a kind of nightmarish drama which also made me wonder if some of the lessons we'd learnt through Elizabeth were all in vain. Mary Craig, in *Blessings*, speaks of the need to re-learn time and again, the lessons taught us through suffering. The truth of this statement was underlined for me at the beginning of the month when I thought I had started a miscarriage.

I was bathing Elizabeth one evening at about 6 p.m. when I became convinced that all was not how it should be. When I had gone into labour with Elizabeth my waters had broken very gradually. It seemed that the same thing was happening again. The difference was that this baby was of twenty-three weeks gestation, with no chance of survival; Elizabeth had been thirty-seven weeks and very healthy.

I telephoned the hospital, shaking all over, and was told to come in. Poor Mark drove us there. Elizabeth was in her night-clothes and a coat, strapped into her car seat. I was in the front seat, clutching a night-dress and crying. It was the same nightmare journey as before. Only for Elizabeth was the significance of the drama lost. She laughed all the way to the hospital, at the novelty of the night-time drive instead of bed. But she was also sick. It was unusual for her to be sick in the evening and I wondered if she sensed our emotions.

I had hardly been able to dress her for the tears streaming down my cheeks. I was shouting at God. Hadn't I learnt enough with Elizabeth? How could losing this baby have any point to it? Why did I have to go through something else like this? I realized as never before how desperately I wished to keep this child. I wanted the chance to have a normal baby.

At the hospital we went into the same waiting-room with the red chairs and rang the bell for a nurse to come. I was shown into a preparation room for an examination. Then the endless wait for a doctor to arrive. Tears ran down my cheeks, I couldn't stop them.

But the sister was confident. They didn't think anything had happened. The doctor would check. Even if the membrane was ruptured, it could heal. I couldn't dare to believe it was a false alarm.

Almost two hours passed before the doctor came and confirmed that I was fine and the baby was safe. I was overjoyed but anxious to tell Mark that all was well. I had crept out earlier to tell him as much as the sister knew, but he was worried. I hated to think of him waiting in the same place that he had waited on that other night nearly two years before, for an event that had then changed our lives.

It took several days to recover from the nightmare of it all. I had made a mistake. But my confidence was at a low ebb. I felt too that I had made an idol out of this hopefully normal child. It seemed more important to me to have this baby than to dare to trust in a loving God who could do as he wished in my life. I didn't want to let go of this baby. Yet somehow I had to, in order to trust God again. I had to begin to feel that whatever the outcome, God would work for good in our lives, as he had done through Elizabeth.

But we had had no choice in having Elizabeth. God had prized from our grasp the idol of 'successful' children and had given us something far more valuable in its place. But we hadn't done it. He had. I would always mind that Elizabeth had a handicap. But God had enabled us to see beyond the externals to more of what life is about. And I was so grateful for Elizabeth.

But I could never not want this second child to be normal and healthy. Perhaps that wasn't what God was saying to me. Maybe what I needed to do was to let God adjust my sights so I could see again that whatever happened to us, he would be there. He would keep us and help us. I had to believe again in a verse from Romans 8 that I was continually having to re-learn: 'All things work together for good for them that love God and are called according to his purpose.'

Mercifully, God did not leave us with only the memory of that anxious evening. Chris reminded me of how planned this second pregnancy had seemed; not by us, but by God. She read from Exodus 23: 'I will send an angel ahead of you to protect you as you travel and to bring you to the place which I have prepared.'

Perhaps because I found it hard at this time to believe in this kind of promise, I discovered something else. Before I went to bed one night I picked up last year's diary that still lay on the bed-side table.

I was amazed to discover, as I leafed through the pages, what emerged about this pregnancy. I remembered in July how a talk with Mark's mother had made me feel more sure that another pregnancy was the right way forward. Several decisions had to be made in the following months regarding Mark's next job. We were conscious each month that God was saying we should wait a little longer until the decisions were made.

Then, the day that I must have conceived this baby was the very day we had the healing service at church. This was the service at which the Sri Lankan Christian spoke and then prayed, amongst many others, for Elizabeth and myself. I had had a real sense of God's presence in that service and now as I looked back I wondered if God was in some way saying, 'This child is part of my healing for Elizabeth and for you.'

It seems significant to me that Elizabeth's conception itself was linked with a healing service that I attended when Mark was at theological college. I decided to ask for prayer for the recurrent cystitis and infections I had found so depressing. Again I felt that God met with us. Not in a dramatic way, but I knew that I had offered this problem to him and I could trust that he would act.

A few weeks later I had a discussion with a friend who was a midwife and she suggested a pregnancy could help to sort out these physical problems. I had a deep-down sense that this was the right way forward. I had lost a baby early on that year, very early in the pregnancy. Now was the time to try again. So Elizabeth's conception too was something we felt was part of God's plan and part of his healing for us. To discover a similar link with the second pregnancy was very encouraging.

As I let the timing of the events sink in, I dared to begin to believe again that God was in control. Gradually my confidence has grown as the baby has grown larger and has moved and kicked. But perhaps it is right that I will never again have that carefree feeling I had in the first months of my pregnancy with Elizabeth when I had little awareness of the problems that could occur.

As the month has worn on the greyness has begun to lift, due partly to seeing Elizabeth make new discoveries. One Sunday afternoon she sat down on the floor with her box of bricks and spent half an hour building. Not just one brick on another, but piles of bricks, three, four, even five bricks high. I was excited. I wondered for how long I had been encouraging her to build bricks. I think it must have been about six months. She had never really been interested and then suddenly this idea had appealed to her and no one could stop her using her new skill. And then she produced her first real word. Although she had said 'Dadda, Mumma, Duck, Tedda' for some time, she rarely used these words and usually only when I nagged her into repetition. But 'down' was different. I couldn't help feeling it was funny that it should be this word, but perhaps my sense of humour is a bit off-beat.

She used 'down' at every opportunity, entirely on her own initiative. She dropped Teddy 'down' from his chair, food 'down' from her high-chair, and later added 'down' at the end of 'Ring-a-ring a roses . . . we all fall. . .' Elizabeth's enjoyment at using this word makes me feel confident that she will talk properly one day, even if it is later than other children.

March. Elizabeth at twenty-three months

As Elizabeth grows older, a new world is slowly opening up for me. With the help of the Open University course, 'The Pre-School Child', I decided to try some new activities for Elizabeth. I made dough and energetically rolled it out, cutting out dogs, trees and stars. Elizabeth enjoyed it too. She helped to push out the shapes and picked and squeezed the dough, trying to roll it and squash it herself. A sand-tray holds fascination for her too; she likes to make patterns in the sand to reveal the red tray beneath.

Painting, jigsaws, more complicated make-believe games are almost imperceptibly becoming interesting activities. She is still tempted to suck the paint brush, but enjoys finger painting. Practise with food has helped this!

Her ability to dance and move to music is increasing and she enjoys stamping on different kinds of floors. I was also surprised to discover that Elizabeth is ready to listen to stories now rather than just to look at picture-books. Her favourite is *The Three Billy Goats Gruff* and she enjoys the different voices of the characters although she always checks to make sure it is only really Mum or Dad and that a real Billy Goat Gruff hasn't slyly crept into the sitting-room.

Elizabeth is becoming more independent, very clearly expressing her views about what she wants to play with and what she wants to eat. For some time she has said 'no' by shaking her head and pushing the object away with her hand. She also said 'yes' by shaking her head but smiling at the same time. It has been fun to encourage her to nod her head instead. She is still obviously proud of her achievement when she gets it right. Very occasionally she has also said 'yeah'.

Another word has developed in connection with food. 'Nanya' began to be used when she wanted a banana, but it applies to other kinds of favourite food too.

In her small pink jumper and plaid skirt she looks very grown-up. I am still surprised to see her progress and develop. And I still always feel grateful. Seeing her sitting on her small chair at her table looking at a book or trying to fit pieces into a jigsaw gives me a great deal of simple pleasure.

Elizabeth, in church, provides amusement too. She

generally spends part of the service reading the hymn-book and climbing onto the pew to wave to the people behind. As the weeks go on she wants to join in more actively, and every time we stand to sing, a small voice joins in enthusiastically by my side.

After the hymn-book and picture-books have been exhausted, she makes desperate attempts to reach the aisle, accompanied by muffled shouts. One day she was kept reasonably happy until just at the end of the service, when she escaped from the pew and ran up the aisle to the altar. On the steps she paused, turned round and grinned broadly at the congregation. I do not find it hard to imagine her on the stage when she is older.

Her other concern in church is to say 'hello' to any babies. Trips along the pews to find customers to touch and speak to are frequent. She often tries to offer hymn-books to her peers, but the response is not always encouraging. They do not seem to appreciate their value as much as Elizabeth does.

This month has been highlighted by Elizabeth's assessment by the educational psychologist. I can see again God's planning the place of Elizabeth's birth. We couldn't have been provided with a more helpful or encouraging person.

I wanted to be prepared for the worst when we went along. I feared being an over-romantic mother, inventing achievements to make myself feel better. But we were delighted that the educational psychologist only confirmed what we had begun to believe about Elizabeth.

He completed another checklist, as well as using the Portage one, and asked Elizabeth to perform a few activities, which she successfully completed. He then said that Elizabeth's general development was close to the average for her chronological age. In some areas she was slightly forward.

The major area of delay was in spoken speech. This was still around the fifteen to eighteen-month level. Potty-training and feeding were also behind, although both seemed to be areas where Elizabeth was currently expressing her independence.

We had expected the verdict on her speech, but I had not expected the encouragement of being told that her level

117

of play was good, particularly her imaginative play, and also that she was a good learner.

Suddenly the two years, which had sometimes been characterized by days of struggling to think up new activities fell into perspective. I felt that we had been enabled to build foundations for the future. We had tried to seize the opportunities we'd had to teach Elizabeth and perhaps now we could relax a little as she began to learn more by herself.

To help her speech I mentioned the idea of teaching reading to teach speech. I knew this had succeeded with some Down's children, because the normal development with speech preceeding reading did not necessarily occur. This was an area still being researched.

I wondered about beginning the 'Teach your baby to read' scheme advocated by Glen Doman, using large red flash cards. New material by Bill Gillham (see bibliography) has also just been published, particularly for Down's children. It was exciting to think about venturing into this new area of language and reading in the next few months.

We ended our interview with a discussion about Elizabeth's future education. The educational psychologist agreed that Elizabeth would continue to learn most through normal playgroups and nursery school. At some point later on she would need some form of special education, but we were to beware of specializing too early. She would possibly benefit too from the early years of a normal infant school, so long as she was given some extra help.

We left the office with relief and joy. We cannot be sure that Elizabeth's development will continue at this rate, but we are just grateful for today. This is the best we could ever have hoped for. Elizabeth has begun to fulfil her potential. We pray we can help her to continue to do so in the future.

17

'Love Was His Meaning'

For us as a family I suppose we are only at the beginning of our story. Perhaps we are at the beginning too of a new struggle: a struggle for acceptance for Elizabeth in our educational system, and in our society.

These last two years have been a time of change, of readjustment, pain and growth, but also of much joy. We have come through a crisis and have learnt how much God is in control for our good. And we have come to know and love deeply a person who has so much to give us.

Yet how easy to forget what we have learnt and to slip back into old ways of thinking. When I caught myself thinking about the arrival of our second child I was suddenly grateful that the event would occur in a new parish and a new area. I could see I would have been tempted to take our second child around to friends, delighting in his or her abilities, and feeling smugly that now we had proved that we could produce a child that reflected our own abilities. Now we were really acceptable. I was glad we wouldn't have that chance. We need situations that help us to rejoice in each person as an individual, greatly loved and valued for themselves.

So we are moving to a new home with a park at the bottom of the garden, and new responsibilities and challenges for Mark. We go, knowing that we leave behind us here two years of experience which we could never repeat and two years in which we have been supported and cared for by a church family which has saved us from the isolation and abnormality that many parents of handicapped children must feel. For this group of people we will always be grateful.

Many people might feel that our own problem with Elizabeth is a very small one compared with others'. Two years is a short time in which to feel we have returned to normality again, even if we will always limp, like Jacob, after he wrestled with God. And Elizabeth herself understands and communicates so much and is little behind the normal at the moment. But perhaps here lies a problem. There is still the prejudice to break down which says 'we don't have handicapped children at this school'. A label can still be a great barrier, even though her ability may at present be very near that of other children her age.

Later on, it is unlikely that she will continue to develop at the same rate. There may be static periods. Physically too she will look a little different. People may be unkind, or take advantage of her.

But we are so conscious of a God of love who has, as Paul wrote in Ephesians 3:20, 'done far more abundantly than all that we ask or think' in answer to our prayers for Elizabeth. God hasn't made her 'normal' or 'like us', but as we have put her into God's hands he has done far more.

The provision of Portage, the playgroup, helpful friends, the support from our own family and the church family, the educational psychologist and plentiful information have been a demonstration to us of God's deep involvement in the structure of our lives. God's love and strength have supported us when it has been hard.

There are questions that we would like to be answered. Questions about the nature of Down's syndrome and its detailed effects on our children. Perhaps some of the questions are being answered by research at the moment and others will be answered in the future. Some we will never know the answer to, but we will go on trying new ideas and methods, hoping for good results.

But people sometimes ask another kind of question. 'Why did this happen to us?' Although we will never fully know the answer, I think we have a few ideas. We needed to have our beliefs in success and acceptability changed radically. Our idols of intellectual excellence and achievement needed to be smashed, not because they are wrong qualities in themselves, but because they have nothing to do with love or a life lived in God's presence and for his glory.

We needed to learn to accept what God allows, believing that he knows what he is doing. And we needed to accept, love and cherish a person simply because of who she is. It isn't hard to do that with Elizabeth. She gives us so much love in return.

If we can continue to learn acceptance, and to relax with who Elizabeth is, not always striving to move her on for our sake, but to help her be as complete a person as she can be, for her own sake, then perhaps we've begun to learn something of what God intended. Elizabeth, for her own confidence in herself to develop, needs our love and acceptance as much as we need to give it.

But in the end, however much we see our eyes opened on to another world, and our hearts and minds humbled by the birth of this special child, perhaps we can only join with Mother Julian of Norwich and say,

You would know our Lord's meaning in this thing? Know it well. Love was his meaning.

Postscript

The summer has come at last and the garden is full of roses. A summer's day has ended with a clear blue sky and tinges of pink and orange between the rooftops.

In a brown wicker cradle lies a little boy. He is just drifting off to sleep. His name is Nicholas. In the next room sleeps a girl who is not quite sure if the advent of this small creature is good or bad. She likes to stroke his head and hands and to hold him but the endless feeds and attention he receives cause her to feel insecure and sad.

But to us, Nicholas has brought a sense of completeness. The two years of a kind of isolation from the world of normality have ended. We are parents as others are parents, without the pain and loss.

Nicholas is healthy and contented. He arrived a week early, quickly and easily. He is someone who will one day be able to understand that he has a special sister.

A few hours after he was born a sudden wave of sadness washed over me, as I realized that Elizabeth could have been like Nicholas. Whole, normal, with the right number of chromosomes. But I pushed away the tears that flowed easily in the aftermath of giving birth. We had been given Elizabeth as a special gift – a kind of bonus child. We can and will rejoice in her. Her smile, perhaps the more appealing because it emphasizes her Down's features, will always bring us joy. She is our special child and Nicholas will one day be grateful that he has known her.

Nicholas Seymour Philps
born 25th May 1983
weight 8lbs
'Unto thee, O Lord, belongs steadfast love.'

Appendix

The Christian Concern for the Mentally Handicapped
118B Oxford Road, Reading, Berks (Tel. 0734 508781).

The charity was established in 1976 by David and Madeline Potter, themselves parents of a Down's syndrome girl.

Aberystwyth
The first property opened with residents in Aberystwyth in 1980. It is linked to Alfred Place Baptist Church and run by a committee of church members. There are sixteen residents, seven care staff, three occupational staff, two voluntary staff.

There is a work-training facility with the aim of training some mentally-handicapped adults for open employment, and others for meaningful work within the workshop. It also provides a place for those who might deteriorate with age and need sheltered work again.

The aim is involvement in the church life and the community.

Expansion
A second home has been opened in Reading for a maximum of twenty residents. Others are opening in Maidstone (for three residents), Deganwy (near Llandudno, North Wales – for four residents) and Bournemouth. Other projects are planned.

Residents
People with varied handicaps and abilities are accepted although a certain measure of social competence is needed so that residents can live with the staff ratio provided. The age range is currently seventeen to fifty-three. Applicants over sixteen are accepted. There are far more applications than places at the moment.

Funding
Capital costs are met by donations. Running costs come from the local authority who sponsor residents and from the DHSS. The 30 per cent shortfall is met by the charity.

This is the only Christian organization that I know of, at present, that has set up a long-term care scheme for mentally-handicapped residents with such strong ties with local churches. These links enable Christian standards to be maintained in the homes and close links to develop with the local community. Because of this, places are much in demand by Christians and non-Christians alike.

Other Establishments

See also: The Directory of Residential Accommodation for the Mentally Handicapped, published by MENCAP 1982. Available at public libraries and from MENCAP.

The Down's Children's Association

The Down's Children's Association is the leading organization for helping parents and professionals with the care, treatment, and training of children with Down's syndrome. It has a resource centre in London and a research centre in Birmingham, a dozen branches and scores of self-help groups. In Scotland its sister organization is the Scottish Down's Syndrome Association.

The DCA was founded in 1970 as a result of the efforts of Rex Brinkworth, a child-psychologist who has demonstrated that Down's children are less handicapped if they are given extra stimulation and training from the very earliest age.

How can the DCA help?
- By encouraging new parents to embark on a detailed programme of stimulation, exercise and diet to bring out the very best in their child – a potential much greater than used to be thought.
- By providing a counselling service for parents at a time of shock and distress.
- By setting up local self-help groups so that parents can share their problems and help each other to adopt a positive approach to solving them.
- By providing information and advice about education, teenage problems, life after school, leaving home and housing.
- By promoting and carrying out research into ways of diminishing the effects of Down's syndrome.
- By creating greater public awareness of the potential of Down's children, a more sympathetic understanding of their needs and greater respect for their right to lead fulfilling and useful lives. The Association believes that the mere possession of Down's syndrome in a new-born baby is not a qualification for it being allowed to die.

For further information, membership details etc, contact:
Miss Maggie Emslie,
Executive Officer,
Down's Children's Association,
4 Oxford Street,
LONDON, W1N 9FL
(Tel. 01–580 0511/2)

Educational Advisor to the Down's Children's Association:
Rex Brinkworth,
The Quinborne Centre,
Ridgacre Road,
Birmingham, B32 2TW
(Tel. 021-427 1374)

Other Helpful Addresses

UK

MENCAP (Royal Society for Mentally Handicapped Children and Adults)
MENCAP National Centre, 123 Golden Lane, London EC1Y 0RT
(Tel. 01-253 9433)

Pre-School Playgroups Association
Alford House, Aveline Street, London SE11 5DJ

Toy Libraries Association
Seabrook House, Wyllyotts Manor, Darkes Lane, Potters Bar, Herts EN6 2HL

British Institute of Mental Handicap
Wolverhampton Road, Kidderminster, Worcestershire DY10 3PP.

Revised MAKATON Vocabulary
published by (Mrs. Margaret Walker, Project co-ordinator) Makaton
Vocabulary Development Project, 85 Pierrefondes Avenue,
Farnborough, Hants.
Makaton is a sign language that has been found to encourage the
development of language in Down's children.

Eire

Down's Syndrome Association of Munster,
Moores Fort, Tipperary

USA

Betty A. Green, Down's Syndrome Congress of California,
5832 Scotwood Drive, Rancho Palos Verdes, California 90274

Australia

Down's Syndrome Association,
PO Box 1556, Brisbane 4001

Association for Developmentally Young Children,
PO Box 379, North Quay, Queensland 4000

Mental Health Centre,
Perth, Western Australia

Queensland Subnormal Children's Welfare Association,
38 Jordan Terrace, Bowen Hills, Brisbane

Subnormal Children's Welfare Association,
8 Junction Street, Ryde, NSW 2112

Mrs Iris Hallam, Co-ordinator for Down's Syndrome,
Darwin Hospital, Casuarina, Darwin, Northern Territory

New Zealand

New Zealand Society for Intellectually Handicapped,
6th Floor, Brandon House, Featherston Street, Wellington

South Africa

Mr M. Botha,
14 Windsor Road, Oostersee, Parow 7500

Italy

Mr Enzo Razzano, Associazione Bambini Down,
Presso Razzano, Largo Boccea 33, Rome

Mexico

Mr J. Alejandro Gonzalez,
Retorno 9 No. 5, Col. Avenue, Mexico 21 D.F.

Bibliography

Ulla Bondo, *Ida*, Faber, 1980; in USA: Merrimack Book Services

Rex Brinkworth and Joseph Collins, *Improving Babies with Down's Syndrome*, Royal Society for Mentally Handicapped Children, Belfast, 1968

Janet Carr, *Young Children with Down's Syndrome*, Butterworth, 1975

Mary Craig, *Blessings*, Hodder and Stoughton, 1979; in USA: William Morrow, 1979; Bantam, 1980

James Copeland with Jack Hodges, *For the Love of Ann*, Arrow, 1973

Cliff Cunningham and Patricia Sloper, *Helping Your Handicapped Baby*, Souvenir Press, Human Horizons Series, 1978; in USA: *Helping Your Exceptional Baby: A Practical and Honest Approach to Raising a Mentally Handicapped Baby*, Pantheon, 1981

Paula D'Arcy, *Song for Sarah*, Lion, 1981; in USA: Harold Shaw, 1979

Bill Gillham, *First Words Language Programme*, Allen and Unwin and Beaconsfield, 1979; in USA: Allen and Unwin and Beaconsfield, 1979

Bill Gillham, *First Words Picture Book*, Methuen, 1982

Bill Gillham, *'First Sentences' Workbooks and Cards*, available from Learning Development Aids, Duke Street, Wisbech, Cambridgeshire, UK

Barry Neil Kaufman, *To Love Is To Be Happy With*, Souvenir Press, Human Horizons Series, 1976; in USA: Fawcett Books, 1978

Fern Kupfer, *Before and After Zachariah*, Gollancz, 1982; in USA: Delacorte Press, 1981

J. R. Ludlow, *Down's Syndrome; Let's Be Positive*, Down's Children's Association, 1980

Gerald Sanctuary, *After I'm Gone*, Souvenir Press, 1984

T. de Vries-Kruyt, *Small Ship, Great Sea*, Collins, 1966

Thomas J. Weihs, *Children in Need of Special Care*, Souvenir Press, Human Horizons Series, 1971; in USA: Schocken Books, 1979

Morris West, *The Clowns of God*, Hodder and Stoughton, 1981, Coronet, 1982; in USA: William Morrow, 1981